BUSINESS PSYCHOLOGY

HOW TO BECOME POWERFUL AND SUCCESSFUL IN BUSINESS

CHRISTIAN D. LARSON

CONTENTS

ABOUT THIS BOOK

This book is a business classic which should be a required reading in every business administration school in the world.

Master of achievement Larson presents us with a masterpiece in business "psychology", as he calls it, which is in reality a treaty and what to do and what to avoid to become a successful business person in the world.

"The foundation of success in the business world is found in the proper combination of enterprise, ability, self-confidence and concentration", says the author, and from there, he takes us in a journey through the rules in Attainment And Achievement; the Science of Business Success and the seven factors that determine Business Success; the use of the mind in practical achievement; the use of the powers of will and desire, and in general, all the elements of business success that have been later copied and explained by other authors.

Larson is the true source of most of this philosophy.

FOREWORD

It is not the purpose of this work to present a complete or extensive study of psychology as applied to the business world; the subject is too large; besides, the majority among practical business men prefer a brief and condensed presentation of the best methods that have been evolved through experiments with business psychology. And it is this preference that has been considered in every chapter.

The practical study of business psychology is of recent origin, but enough has been worked out in this vast field to justify the making of almost any claim for its value that psychology itself declares to be within the bounds of the possible. And this is saying a good deal, because thus far neither limit nor end has been found to the possibilities of the psychological side.

The psychological side is invariably the most important side, and everything has a psychological side. The psychological side of the business world is now recognized by all wide-awake business men, and they all admit with pride, that practically all the great improvements that have recently been made, both in the building of business and in the building of more efficient business men, have sprung directly from the study of business psychology. The study of this subject, therefore, is not a novelty ; on the contrary, it has become a necessity.

The business man, however, has very little time for extensive or technical study; a work on business psychology therefore should be directly to the point in every respect, and should present the greatest amount of practical information possible in the least space possible. In the following pages a special effort has been made to comply with this requirement; so that where brevity may seem to be too conspicuous, everybody will know the cause.

Special attention has been given to the possibility of evolving an exact business science, a science which when applied would bring success with a certainty; and the aim has been to permeate every page with the spirit of this possibility, which is fast becoming an actuality—first, that success can be realized by all men of push, enterprise and efficiency, and second, that all those factors in the human mind that produce success, when applied, can be developed and perfected to almost any degree imaginable, which means that greater success can be realized in any field, by those who will pay the price, than has ever been realized before.

No attempt has been made to work out some definite system through which the principles of business psychology might be applied in the various fields of the commercial and industrial worlds. For again the subject is too large to be treated exhaustively in a small volume. The object, therefore, has been to present as many ideas and methods as space would permit, giving each reader the privilege to evolve his own system— course that all progressive business men will prefer. And that the application of these ideas will increase decidedly the success of any man is a fact of which we are positively convinced.

1

LAWS AND METHODS THAT INSURE SUCCESS.

In the past the study of psychology was purely speculative. It had no definite object in view. Its attention was devoted almost exclusively to a general study of mental phenomena, but no thought was given to the possible effect of such phenomena. It did not study the mind itself, nor were attempts made to determine what effect the movements of the mind might have upon the practical side of everyday life. Psychology therefore was something that was more or less intangible, something that was largely theoretical, something that was looked upon as far removed from the field of personal action. For this reason such terms as practical psychology or business psychology could have no significance whatever; but in this respect, as well as in many other respects, things have changed remarkably in recent years.

We now know that all psychology is practical or can be made practical, and that the most important side of everything in the world of practical action is the psychological side. It is therefore evident that there must be a business psychology. In fact, a business psychology is absolutely necessary because it is the psychology of business that makes it possible for the business itself to live, grow and develop. This, however, many business men do not realize, while the majority of those who have come to this realization, do not clearly understand the actual purpose nor the possible power of the psychological element./. They know that it is the psychology of the thing, or rather the way in which the psychological side is employed that determines results, but they do not have a clear idea as to how the psychological side can be directed or employed to the best advantage. But as this understanding is absolutely necessary if the desired results are to be secured, with a certainty, it is evident that the need of a business psychology is very great to say the least.

To achieve success in the largest possible measure is the life-long ambition of every wide-awake business man, and therefore he refuses, and justly so, to give his attention to those things through which his success may not be promoted. Though in his enthusiasm to pursue what is usually spoken of as successful business methods, he has overlooked the most important of all; that is, he has practically ignored the psychology of business, not knowing its nature or value.

He has instead given his attention almost exclusively to what is usually spoken of as more practical subjects, but here We meet a large question.

What is it that makes a subject practical, and what are the things that really make for success? The average business man is unable to give the answer. In fact, most business men have never thought seriously of this subject. The average business man believes that the principal secrets to success are found in hard work, enterprise, economy, safe investments and an abundance of good luck. But here we may well ask why the great majority of business men do not succeed as well as they might wish, regardless of the fact that they follow all the rules of the captains of business that have gone before.

We also might ask in the same connection why the reason is that such an enormous amount of waste is constantly taking place in nearly every industrial establishment. It is a well-known fact that the waste, both in production and distribution, is enormous, and we know that the business man does not wish it to be so. He is daily losing through such channels, but why does he permit these losses to continue if he is fully convinced that he is in possession of the real secrets of business success?

When we note the many mistakes that are made even by the leaders in the commercial world, and how the great majority are almost constantly standing in their own light, we may be pardoned for doubting the idea that modern business has been made a science, and that exact methods have been found for securing success. People who are not in direct contact with the business world are frequently told to imitate modern business methods if they would succeed, and to establish themselves upon the same sound principles if they would achieve something worthwhile. But what are those principles? Who can tell us? It is a fact that the average business man is unable to state definitely what principles he considers to be at the basis of a successful business. Then we may be permitted to ask how modern business can be so very sound, realizing the fact that the majority fail to get more than a bare living out of it, and also that a considerable number of those who achieve great success, as the world measures success, frequently employ methods that are not justifiable.

There are a great many very successful business men who have achieved their success through legitimate means only, but when we analyze the lives of those men we find that they did not succeed through the use of what is usually termed modern business methods. They knew something about the psychology of business or they employed the principal elements of business psychology, possibly without using this term, or without knowing the exact nature of the principles employed.

It is not the purpose here to find fault with business methods, or to criticize anything in any shape or form, but it is a fact that when we thoroughly examine all those methods that are directly connected with modem business, and then at the same time examine closely the nature and the workings of the human mind in all its phases, we invariably come to the conclusion that business as it has been conducted up until recent years has been a hopeless mixture of unscientific schemes and bungling methods. We are speaking, of course, of business in general. There are many noble exceptions, and it is these noble exceptions that give the commercial world what stability it is known to possess. However, when speaking of modern business and modern business methods we do not refer to the progressive business of this age, but to that phase of business that is gradually passing as it is giving away to the coming of business psychology. And we simply mention the methods and the principles of that form of business that is passing, in order to produce a more definite contrast with the new idea of business; that is, a business that will be strictly scientific, or that is, based upon the principles of business psychology.

It is a well-known fact that the commercial world is one of the prime essentials in the promotion of the welfare of man, and therefore it ought to be conducted upon the very best principles possible; and should accordingly employ methods through which the very best results, and only the best results, may be secured; but to make this possible we must go back of effects. We must go back of mere business itself and find the power that is in it all. This power we know to be the mind of man, and the study of mind is called psychology. Therefore the study of the human mind as related to the business world, and as directly applied in the business world, will naturally be termed business psychology.

The mind has many phases; therefore, there are many phases of psychology, in fact, as many kinds as there are individualized uses for the mind; and as the mind is the principal factor in commercial achievements we naturally conclude that a thorough knowledge of such psychology must be indispensable to him who would succeed in business, or who aims to secure the greatest results through his efforts wherever those efforts may be applied.

When we examine what is usually termed success in the commercial world, we come to the conclusion that such success depends directly upon ability, self-confidence, concentration and enterprise. It is with these factors, therefore, that we must begin, as these are fundamental, though there are scores of others that will have to be considered in a complete study of this subject. At the very outset every business man must possess these four essentials if he would be successful in a true and a lasting sense.

But to secure these essentials he must study business psychology; that is, he must study the use of the mind in business. If he already has these essentials he must, in order to secure the best results, understand the use of the mind because a factor is of no value no matter how well it is developed until it is scientifically applied. In either case, therefore, practical psychology becomes indispensable.

In the past, the idea was simply to proceed to use your ability as well as you knew how, without giving any attention whatever to the principles and laws that govern the use of that ability. In brief, the use of talent, or practical ability along any line was continued in some helter-skelter fashion, and when success was secured it was counted good luck. Times, however, have changed. Now we know, that good luck is simply the result of scientific application and that it may be created by man himself, provided he knows how to use himself or apply himself.

The wise business man today does not proceed in any way that happens to be convenient. He insists upon understanding the scientific way so as to get definite results and the desired results from every move he makes. He is not satisfied to simply say that brains and ability will insure success. He knows that a man may have plenty of brains and any amount of ability and never succeed because it is not only an essential to possess those factors that are needed in success—^we must also know how to use those factors.

The majority do not know how to use their brains to the best advantage, nor do they know how to use their mental and physical energies. This is proven by the fact that the average person wastes more energy than he applies in his work, and also that most of his faculties are never applied to full capacity. We are all aware of the fact that there are thousands of men and women with fine brains and splendid abilities who go through their work every day, making mistakes at every turn, and who go through life without accomplishing anything really worthwhile. And the cause of this is found in the fact that the science of practical application has not been studied; in other words, those men and women have not become familiar with business psychology.

To have a fine brain is absolutely necessary and a good mind is indispensable, but brain and mind do not control themselves. We must know how to make exact and scientific use of these things if we are to accomplish what we have in view. How to use the mind according to system, law and scientific method—that is what constitutes practical psychology. And the importance of this subject is becoming so great that the day is fast approaching when it win be taught in all universities. In the meantime the man who would succeed according to full capacity must seek this knowledge from every available source, and must never cease his study.

When men and women proceed in life to do their share in science, art, industry or civilization they should have principles upon which to base their work, and such principles as would assure constant advancement Even though the advancement be slow it is nevertheless true that so long as you understand the principles of advancement and apply those principles you will continue to move forward. And he who continues to move forward is already meeting with success. But in the average mind there is no certainty as to how to proceed in order to move forward continuously. When a man proceeds to dig a ditch he knows that the ditch will continue to grow longer so long as he applies the spade. In his mind there is no doubt as to the outcome of his work. But in the mind of the average business man there is constant doubt. He does not know what the results will be, and therefore his methods are not nearly as scientific as the methods of the man in the ditch. This, however, is not complimentary to the supposed superior intelligence of the business man, though the cause of this uncomplimentary position is found in the fact that the business man does not understand the principles upon which he works. He proceeds usually in a helter-skelter fashion and is not certain as to whether he is building for greater things or is moving toward failure.

The majority today do not know where they will be tomorrow. They do not know whether they will be in poverty or in some unexpected good fortune, and most of them live constantly in a subconscious dread of reverses. Their minds are therefore under a cloud, and no mind can do its best under such conditions. It is evident, therefore, that we must proceed along different lines in the commercial world. We must try to find those principles through which we know success can be attained with a certainty, provided, of course, that we continue to apply those principles with the same enthusiasm as the man applies his strength upon the spade who is working in the ditch.

If we aim to produce great men and women, and to secure the greatest achievements possible from the efforts of such men and women, we must give them methods through which the mind may always be at its best regardless of circumstances or advers-ityj5 and methods that will always produce the desired results when applied, regardless of the conditions that may prevail. And to present such methods is the purpose of practical psychology. In fact, practical psychology can give us principles, laws or methods that will positively insure success. Anyone who will apply such methods will move forward. He will advance every year just as certainly as the rising of the sun. So long as he applies the principles of practical psychology he will gain ground steadily, and his success will increase from year to year. In fact, there is one thing that he is positively assured of, and that is success, a continued and constantly increasing success. If his ability is limited, his advancement in the beginning will be slow, but since he can yearly increase his ability, the advancement from year to year will become more rapid in proportion. However, if his ability is very great, his advancement from the beginning will be remarkable and will constantly increase as he continues the further development of that ability. Here we have a solid foundation for sound business, and it is established upon the scientific use of mind and ability according to such requirements as are demanded in the commercial world.

Any man or woman, therefore, who will find the work that is most suitable for the talents possessed, may, through the application of practical psychology be assured of a real, a constant and an ever increasing success. And in this connection it is well to remember that business psychology can also aid the individual in finding that work for which he is best adapted.

Such statements as we must inevitably make when examining the possibilities of practical psychology may seem to be too strong to be based upon absolute fact. But the question is, cannot any mathematical problem be worked out when we know the principles, the laws, and the methods involved? We admit that it can. Then why should not this rule hold everywhere.

Every successful business man in the world has achieved his success through the right use of his mental faculties at the right place and at the right time. We must conclude, therefore, that when we learn to use our talents in the right way, at the right time and in the right place, we shall also have the right results. This everybody will of course admit. But is it always possible to act rightly at the right time and place? This may not always seem possible, but here, as elsewhere, the rule holds that difficult things seem impossible only until we know how. When we know how the most difficult becomes most simple.

The wise man, however, does not stand back and call such things impossible as he does not understand. On the contrary, he comes forward and demands the desired information. If there is anything better to be had he wants it, and such men always get it. The man who has his eyes open, who is always looking for the best that is to be had, that is the man who always gets the best. Accordingly, he steadily rises in the scale, while those who are constantly being frightened by the word "impossible** continue to lag behind, wondering in the meantime why some people have such good luck, and others have not.

The wise man does not require tangible demonstrations to prove a valuable idea. You do not have to show him effects in order to prove the value of the cause. When you give him a good idea he knows that that idea is good, and that if applied will produce good results. Accordingly, he does not wait for somebody else to produce the results. He proceeds to produce those results himself and thereby reaps the benefit of a very valuable principle employed at the psychological moment. Those, however, who wait for somebody else to prove the value of the idea do not take advantage of the psychological moment, and therefore miss a great opportunity.

We see these things taking place every day, and it simply proves that the successful business man must change his tactics and must try to gain a deeper understanding of those laws and principles that underlie results in the commercial world. It is only in this way that he can meet the growing demands of advancement and continue to be up in front, regardless of how rapid the progress of the world may be. And most business men in this age realize this great fact. They realize that something else is needed besides the old methods to insure success in the commercial world. They know that success depends upon the man himself, the mind

that the man possesses, and the way the faculties of that mind are employed. They also appreciate the many aids to success that are to be found in knowing how to detect and take advantage of opportunities that are constantly passing by. But beneath all of this they realize that there must be a real science of business, a science that any man can learn, a science which, if faithfully applied, must with a certainty produce results desired in every case. And all that is necessary to add in this connection is that such a science must inevitably be the natural outcome of a thorough study and a thorough application of the principles of practical psychology

2

THE FOUR GREAT ESSENTIALS TO BUSINESS SUCCESS.

The foundation of success in the business world is found in the proper combination of enterprise, ability, self-confidence and concentration. True, there is a superstructure; there is a lower story and an upper story, and several other stories intervening, all of which we must consider in their proper places.; But the foundation must be considered first, and in doing so our object will be to present the psychological side of all these factors, and prove that the psychological side is not only the principal side, but that a thorough understanding of the psychological side will make success just as certain as the rising of the sun."

When we speak of enterprise the average mind naturally thinks of hustle, push, more work and eternally being at it, but we shall find that this term also involves something else, the understanding of which will be of incalculable value to everybody in the business world. To adopt the rule of more work is necessary, as nothing is accomplished without much work, but simply to resolve to work is not everything in work.

There is an art of working. There is constructive enterprise and destructive enterprise. There is work that promotes your objects and there is work that simply wastes time and energy. In fact, misdirected work is so common that it is met by nearly everybody every hour. If some method, therefore, could be found that would enable every intelligent person to direct his work properly at all times, one of the greatest secrets of success would have been revealed. To strike the nail on the head every time is the purpose of work. But in too many instances the man with the hammer crushes his own thumb.

To define work we may say that it is physical or mental action applied through certain channels for the purpose of producing certain intended results. The work itself is force or energy practically applied, but the results do not depend altogether upon how much energy is employed. Results also depend upon the way the energy is employed. However, that something that directs all energy in work is not to be found in the muscles, nor in the senses, nor even in the ordinary exterior intellect. This something belongs to the very finest elements of the mind and the study of these things constitutes one of the principal fields of the new psychology.

There is, therefore, a psychological side to work, and no work can be done properly without a knowledge of this side. It is a well-known fact that your mental attitude toward your work does just as much for success or failure as the work itself, and also that your states of mind while at work determine largely how much energy you will be able to give to your work. For this reason we realize the importance of the psychological side. To enter into details and present the mental laws involved in this subject will not be necessary, however, but it will be necessary to say that no one can afford to be ignorant of the psychological side of work, because no matter how hard he may work or how much energy he may possess, as long as he does not understand the mental laws involved most of his efforts will be misdirected. The subject, therefore, becomes important and will be given proper attention in the proper place.

Passing to the study of ability we find a theme as large as life itself and containing possibilities too large to be measured. It has been well said that the man with brains can do anything he may set out to do, and can secure practically anything he may wish for. But though this is a great truth it offers no consolation to those who are not in possession of remarkable brains. These people, however, need not be discouraged because brains can be developed. Accordingly, there is no excuse any more for having a small mind, or for being deficient in ability or capacity along any line. These things can all be developed to almost any degree desired, and exceptional improvements secured in a short time. We naturally conclude, therefore, that before every mind lies a path of unlimited possibilities.

The average person, however, has not given much attention to the increase of his ability. He has labored under the conviction that no increase was possible and has depended upon the application of what ability he possessed through the channel of hard work. Here, then, is a new field for men and women who desire progress in the world of achievement. To carry out this idea we must not rush headlong with the crowd, expecting to arrive through the lucky application of our present capacity. On the contrary, we must give just as much attention to the increase of our ability as to the practical use of that ability.

At first sight, however, it may seem that success will be interfered with by such a method, as the average person thinks that he needs all of his time for practical work and what ability he has must be put into that work. For this reason he believes that he has neither the time nor the opportunity, but the fact is that every man who wants to can find the necessary time for improvement. That this is a fact will be evident when we realize that the mind will not be tired out after a day's work when we learn to work in the right mental attitude; and also that development will be continuous, even while we are at work, provided we work through right mental actions.

Every man, whether he has been in business for many years or is just beginning, should make it a point to give a certain amount of time and attention every day to the further development of those faculties that are directly involved in his work. More brains must be his leading purpose and his constant desire, and where there is a will there is a way. By adopting this method he may not in the beginning be able to give his work as much attention as he planned, though in most instances he will be able to give it all the attention required. After a short time, however, he will begin to become a greater power in his field of action, and will find himself able to do better work and more work in less time.

In all efforts quality should be sought first, though the average person sets out with his whole attention fixed upon quantity. And here we have one reason why so many fail to accomplish anything of worth.

After you have resolved to give a certain amount of time and attention to the further increase of your personal ability, impress your mind with the fact that the faculties or talents that you employ in your work can be developed indefinitely. Realize this fact so fully that you feel it at all times. To feel inwardly that your ability can be enlarged indefinitely will of itself produce an increase of capacity every moment. And when you apply in conjunction a good system of practical methods the results will be steady and wholly satisfactory.

In this connection it is absolutely necessary to break away from the old habit of being absolute slave to your business; you must always rule your work, and not permit yourself to be ruled by your work under any circumstances. To develop the mind, the mind must not only be free from all conditions and circumstances, but must be the master of them all. And in carrying out this principle we shall find it necessary to possess an abundance of self-confidence, the third essential to real success.

We may have more brains than we can use, but if we have no faith in ourselves we shall accomplish but little. That this is true we all know because we are all acquainted with fine minds who do not believe in themselves and who therefore undertake nothing. Many of these could startle the world if they believed that they could, though where faith and self-confidence are lacking there is no incentive whatever to make any definite attempt along any definite line. Where faith is abundant a little ability will go a long way, and some of the most successful men in the world owe their great results to self-confidence, as their ability is in many instances below the average.

The great power of self-confidence lies in the fact that when you believe that you can do certain things all the power of your being accumulates in those faculties through which the work is to be done. When you thoroughly believe that you can accumulate wealth you draw all the energy of your system into that part of the brain through which the financial faculties function. When you believe with all your mind that you can write a great work of fiction all your literary faculties will become alive with energy, coming in from all parts of mind and personality. The same is true along any line where your self-confidence and your faith in yourself has become very strong. This is why faith is so remarkable, and why self-confidence is indispensable.

True, if you have no ability for the work which you believe you can do, there will be no results for the time being. Energy must have something to work with, even though that something be small. But even though it should be small at first, that faculty will grow with great rapidity when all the forces of your being begin to accumulate there. Therefore, to believe that you can do what you have no ability for, will be useless. Self-confidence alone cannot produce results, but when you know that you have some ability in a certain direction, and everybody has ability in one or more directions, give this ability all the self-confidence you can possibly arouse. Proceed with the full use of that faculty and believe that you can accomplish anything with it The results will be remarkable. Through such a believe and through such an application this faculty will grow so rapidly that ere long you will be able to do far more than you first expected.

The law is that when we believe we can do certain things all the creative forces in our system will rush into the faculty required to do the thing we have planned. This added power will constantly increase the capacity of that faculty so that in the course of time it will possess remarkable ability. In the average person the various creative forces of his system are scattered all through the system and are mostly thrown away through lack of use; but if all of these energies could be gathered in the one place in the mind it is evident that far more could be accomplished, and this is what happens when self-confidence is strong. The nature of faith and self-confidence is to draw everything along with it into those faculties that are being used for the work at hand. Accordingly, self-confidence converts enemies into friends and uses obstacles as stepping stones. However, to develop faith and self-confidence we must understand the laws of mind and soul, and that involves the study of psychology.

The fourth great essential is that of concentration, and the purpose of concentration is to hold attention upon the work at hand as long as may be required. There are a few minds that can think of one thing and continue to think of one thing for hours and feel no fatigue, but the average mind can keep his attention upon one subject for a moment only, and when he does try to concentrate for some time he becomes mentally exhausted. One reason for this is found in the belief that concentration necessarily involves hard mental work, and that we must force the mind to hold it in a concentrated attitude. This, however, is not the truth.

When concentration is natural no effort at all is required, and in natural concentration you do not try to fix the attention, nor try to hold the mind in place. You simply become interested in your subject or your work. When you are deeply interested in something you naturally concentrate upon that something without making any special effort to do so. And so long as your interest continues your mind will give its whole attention in that direction.

But here the question is how we shall become interested in such things that we care nothing about, for we may be called upon to do things we dislike and the doing of those very things may be stepping stones to what we shall like. But we cannot do that work successfully unless our concentration is good. Thus the problem is how to concentrate upon that which we dislike, or how to become interested in that in which we have no interest. To this problem, however, there is a simple solution.

When we work with a purpose in view we look beyond the mere work. We look upon the work as the path to the coveted goal, and in this light our work means everything to us. Accordingly, we cannot help being deeply interested in it, knowing what we are to find at the end of the journey.

When we work simply to make a living and do not use our work as a means to higher attainment, in addition to the making of a livelihood, we may find it difficult to be interested in it. But when we look upon our work as a means to a great end we shall find no difficulty whatever in becoming interested in every step of the way. We shall then enter our work with joy and be animated with a strong desire to do it in the very best way possible.

When we proceed in this manner our interest in our work will be constant, and accordingly we will develop natural concentration. Ere long concentration will become highly developed so that we can give our whole mind and all our creative forces*to the one thing we are doing now, and for any length of time without feeling the least mental weariness. This is a very simple method, a method that anybody can apply, and if applied faithfully will develop concentration in any mind, even to a remarkable degree.

When these four essentials have been secured or developed the next important step is to attain resourcefulness, and this may, figuratively speaking; be called the first story of the superstructure.

When we examine the average mind we find it to be just so much, and no matter how long you may know that mind you will never see any more in it. New things are not brought to the surface and the mental resources are so limited that you can see them all by looking at the surface of the mind. A person with such a mind has no agreeable surprises in store for anybody. He is what he appears to be, and no more. Such a person, however, will never startle the world with great achievements, nor even live a life satisfactory to himself unless he becomes familiar with the new psychology and applies its principles.

To accomplish much the mind must come into touch with the limitless source of ideas, thoughts and experiences. In other words, we must find that place in consciousness where the elements of construction are stored away in boundless supply; and the resourceful mind has found this place. For this reason the resourceful mind is never at its ** wits-ends," it is never at a loss, it is never without a way. Such a mind simply opens itself to the thing needed and it comes. We call such a mind resourceful, but we have not in the past known the secret.

All great minds have this faculty naturally developed, and use it unconsciously; that is, they use it without knowing its true nature and without knowing how to increase its power. We all know such people, and that resourcefulness is one of their strong qualities is common knowledge. But can we all attain the same? The answer is that we can, and the fact is that we must. In these days when so many new things are appearing and so many new possibilities are being revealed, the mind must live very near to the limitless in order to take advantage of everything, as well as to continue in the front ranks.

The art of developing the faculty of resourcefulness takes us deeper into psychology than almost any other study along this particular line, as it is the subconscious mind that must be dealt with. To awaken the great within is the one essential; that is, to expand consciousness so that it can take in at least a part of that immense mental field that lies back of ordinary waking consciousness. Psychologists all admit that the ordinary field of consciousness is but a fraction of the immense field of the subconscious, and though a few minds have succeeded in exploring this region to some extent, it is to the average mind a closed door.

The limitations of most minds is due to the fact that the subconscious has not been explored and developed, while the remarkable resourcefulness we find among a number of the larger minds is caused directly by the awakening of some one or two phases of the great within. When the subconscious begins to act new ideas become very numerous, and in many instances new plans come in such great numbers that you do not really know which one to choose. Sometimes all of them are so good that it is next to impossible to say which one is best.

In this experience the mind must be well poised and mutt stand firmly between the outer and the inner, so as to know how to apply the external needs with the best adapted idea or plan from within. At times minds in this state become so confused from their many ideas that they remain inactive for a time. To overcome this condition we must develop a keen insight and also develop continuity so that we will finish whatever we undertake. However, it is from the great within that all genius, all inspiration, all truth and all remarkable constructive power is evolved. Therefore, we cannot give the subject too much attention if we wish to become much and achieve much.

In practical every-day life we constantly come to places where we do not know what to do next, and accordingly suffer failure because we are not prepared for the emergency; but this could never have happened if the immense inner world had been awakened, and we had been in possession of resourcefulness. In the awakening of the within there are many steps, but the first one is to train the mind to look deeper than the surface no matter what the thought or action may be. This practice will in a very short time begin to produce results, though when results come the mind should be well poised and as clear as crystal in order that it may accept the best ideas as they appear. As in all other things it is practice that makes perfect, and he who proceeds with a view of securing great results will certainly secure them.

When we speak of these inner laws of the mind the very practical man may think that the subject is too transcendental to be of any value in commercial life, but let no one fall into this error. We all know that building capacity, as well as all ideas of value, come from the deeper realms of mind and thought, and since everything follows definite laws, there must also be laws for bringing forth, not only greater capacity and ability, but also as many new ideas, plans, methods and principles as may be required to make the work of any mind highly successful. And as it is these laws with which business psychology is chiefly concerned, it is evident that the man who studies and applies the principles of business psychology will place himself in the most advantageous position that can be found in the commercial world.

3

GENERAL RULES IN ATTAINMENT AND ACHIEVEMENT

True success is the natural inheritance of every ambitious mind, and to succeed in every undertaking should be the ceaseless aim of every person And this aim cannot be too high. The fact is the majority underrate their ability . in nearly every instance, therefore never accomplish much more than one-half of what they might. True success, however, is not measured by mere money, but also by personal worth, ability, real greatness, and the doing of things that are difficult, or of great value to the world.

The successful man has done what others before him could not do. Accordingly, he has made the world richer and better and has become an example for millions to follow. Every man that succeeds becomes a model for the race, and his methods become patterns for many generations. The successful man seeks to become something and to do something, and he does not ignore anything, however trivial it may seem, that may be conducive to his growth and advancement.

In this connection a few general rules may be presented in attainment and achievement, rules that will be found of exceptional value to every one who has real success in view. But here it must be remembered that the true conception of success is as broad as the powers of man, and that the gains that naturally follow such a success may include everything that has value and worth, everything that heart can wish for, everything that the mind can use«

Of all rules the most fundamental is this, that all true success depends upon yourself. Therefore to make yourself more competent as well as greater in every sense of the term must be the first essential. Improve yourself and aim to gain in knowledge, power and insight every day. Aim to develop a strong mind, a steady and strong personality and a powerful character, as all of these are great essentials.

In this connection, however, the complaint is frequently made that people who work have little time for study or self-improvement, and though this may be true in some cases it is by no means the rule. The fact is that if the average person, especially the younger person, would eliminate useless pleasures and devote that extra time to self-improvement, a change for the better, and in many cases a remarkable change, would be realized in a few years. The young man or young woman who is after real success and true greatness must say farewell to useless amusements. But this should not be looked upon as a sacrifice, because in truth such a course would mean gain. Look at yourself, therefore, and your habits, then eliminate all those things in your life that are useless, that simply waste time, and you will find abundance of time to give to your own cultivation and advancement.

The old saying, "Let young people have a good time while they are young for it will not last long,*' is too absurd to remember for a moment If you live right and constantly improve yourself you will enjoy life every day as long as you live. That young people, therefore, should waste their time on cheap and useless pleasure, and that people of more years should live a dejected and uninteresting life, is an idea that does not belong to this age of wisdom and light.

The new rule is to use your time well while you are young and you will remain young; and what is more, you will be something in the world. The question is not whether we should enjoy ourselves, for we all must have pleasure every day. The question is, shall we continue to live a small, cheap life with nothing but the commonest of pleasures, when we can learn to live a large, rich life that will ever be full to overflowing with the very best that the world can give. This is the question, and every ambitious mind will give the right answer.

One of the first rules, therefore, is to begin today and arrange to carry on a systematic course of self-improvement, embracing as many branches as time and present ability will permit.

Another important rule is to associate only with the successful, the industrious and the aspiring. The people we seek as companions have a marked effect upon us. Therefore, if they are pessimistic, believing in nothing but poverty, failure and injustice, you have nothing to gain and much to lose by seeking their association. But there is no reason why we should seek the association of such people. There are any number of great souls in the world so that we can find as many as we may desire for companions.

Above all, have faith in yourself. It is better to overrate than to underrate yourself. Know that you can succeed; thus you will speak and act accordingly. Expect great things of yourself and continue to expect such things until they are realized. Stand upon your own feet, but live closely to minds and souls that have achieved much. Believe that the bright side will prevail, and in the midst of darkness know that better moments are at hand when the sun will shine again.

Draw the bright side of things into your life by a persistent faith in the supreme power of everything that is good; but do not simply desire the bright side of life. Live such a life yourself. The importance of this may be well illustrated by taking two men of equal ability and opportunity, but the one habitually cheerful, while the other habitually morose. In the world of success the former has ten times the chance of the latter. We all seek the sunny soul, both in society and in business. The cheerful man will attract where the sullen man will repel, and in the realms of attainment the power to attract good things is a matter of enormous importance. But cheerfulness has a greater value than this. Cheerfulness is constructive and accumulative. All good things come to the man who is ever bright and happy, for remember that it is sunshine that makes things grow.

Make it a point never to talk or think of failure or adversity. Be determined to succeed, and permit no thought or word to suggest anything else, no matter if things today seem to go wrong. At such times remember the great statement, "This shall also pass away." The fact is that the world is always your friend, even though some parts of it may seem at times to be against you. Though when the world does seem to be against you, remember the reason is that you have not met the world in the right way.

Change yourself. Be a friend to everybody—the whole world. Expect everybody to be good to you and desire constantly to be of real service to the human race, and you shall find ere long that fate will change. When you believe that everybody is against you, you rub them all the wrong way, so therefore the blame is upon you alone. Know that the true side of mankind is a true friend to every aspiring soul. Then place yourself in touch with the ideal in man. Meet only his better side, and your life, as well as the life of the world, will be made richer thereby.

Make it the rule of your life to think success, to speak success, to breathe success, to attract success, to live success, and to be saturated through and through with absolute faith in your own success. Believe with your whole heart that the whole world is for you, and that nothing is against you. Then you will find that as your faith is, so shall it be.

At the present time there are thousands of people who believe they are in bondage to the present system of competition and they think of themselves as slaves to this system, but they are simply demonstrating the law that he who is for captivity into captivity goes. He who believes that he is a slave to any system will become a slave to that system according to his belief. It is true that the present social and industrial order can be improved, but we are not helping ourselves nor society by acting the roll of slaves and weaklings. Society and industry will better themselves as mankind raises himself to a higher level, and every time it passes from the attitude of serfdom to the attitude of mastership will, in a measure, lift up the whole world thereby. When you believe yourself to be a slave to the powers that be you simply forge your own fetters, but when you believe yourself to be a master over yourself, a master over your conditions, a master over your own attainment and achievement, you will gradually gain mastership over all those things, and ere long everything will begin to come your way.

Never live in the attitude of inferiority, and never permit yourself to appear as an inferior being. Both mind and body should be well dressed, especially the mind. If you look common, you will think of yourself as common, and he who thinks of himself as common will become common. To present a good appearance need not involve extra expense. It costs no more to be neat, clean and presentable than to be otherwise, though the gain is very great. The fact is that nothing that has a tendency to make you reckless about yourself or your appearance will awaken mind, character and ability. Give special attention, therefore, to the dressing of the mind. And we all can dress the mind in the most perfect manner imaginable.

To proceed, no thought of inferiority should ever enter the mind. On the contrary, think of yourself as a superior being. Think constantly of greatness that is in you and claim it as your own. Live, think and act as if you were somebody, because you are. All that is great and wonderful is latent in your own soul. Such an attitude, however, need not imply an external display of egotism, for the fact is that he who has found his true greatness will be modest and reserved in his external life; but his internal life will be a life with great power; and in the secret places of his own mind he knows what he is.

In this connection, know that you have a mission in life. Believe positively that your work is important, that the world needs you and that you must do your best. Do not associate mentally, however, with the coldness and heartlessness of the perverted side of live. Continue to live mentally with the better side of man. Associate and work only with those who are upward bound, and think only of the strong and the great. Then remember that adversities to you are but opportunities for demonstrating the greater power that is in you, and as you proceed in this attitude you will always be buoyant with life, joy and power, and the ship of your life will continue to sail on.

To proceed with the fuller application of these ideas it will be necessary to give special attention to the new idea of work, ability, and faith. These are most important factors and where properly combined, failure becomes impossible. How to work, how to apply ability, how to develop greater ability, how to secure faith, and how to use faith—these are problems that demand solution from all minds that would rise in the scale of life. But these solutions are not difficult to find, the fact is they are within easy reach of any mind, and therefore we can state positively that anyone can succeed.

It is a well-known fact that competent men and women are in great demand everywhere, but it is not clear to the average person what it means to be competent, nor is it generally known that practical ability can be developed. According to the old idea the mind with ability might succeed, while the mind without ability would have to be satisfied with what little the limitations of his mind might be able to produce. This idea, however, is not true in any sense of the term and should be eliminated completely.

Any person can improve himself when he knows how, and anyone can learn how. Though you may be wholly incompetent today, next year you may be able to fill a responsible position and be on the way to a great and ever-growing success, for there is nothing to hinder the advancement of anyone after he has learned the secret, and has resolved not to stand in his own way anymore.

To succeed means to move forward, and as all forward movements depend upon constructive efforts all work must be constructive. But work must not simply be constructive, it must be constructive to the very highest degree. And here is where ability becomes indispensable. Too much of the work that is done in the world is a mere waste of time and energy. It is simply taking the haystack from one hill to another without increasing the amount of hay or adding to the welfare of those who do the moving.

The amount of waste that is going on in the business world is startling to say the least, though we do not have to look far to find the cause. Lack of ability and insight are invariably the causes, and since the average person has in the past doubted both the existence of insight and the possibility of improvement in himself, we can readily understand why this waste has continued. When we examine the lives of very successful men we find that they had a happy faculty of doing the right thing at the right time; and we also find that this happy faculty combined with considerable ability and a strong desire for work, was the real secret of their great success.

But what is this happy faculty of doing the right thing at the right time ? It is simply insight; that is, an extraordinary power of mind to penetrate into the forces, circumstances and conditions of industrial or commercial life. We may call it foresight or we may define it as being long-headed, but whatever our definition may be the faculty remains the same, and we know it is a superior and much-needed faculty. Modern psychology has discovered that this great faculty is faith in practical action, and also that this faculty will steadily develop so long as we exercise continuous faith in conjunction with practical action.

But what is faith ? We have been so in the habit of thinking of faith as a mere belief in something that cannot be proven that it will be necessary to employ both persistence and mental discipline to establish in our minds the correct view. Faith is a mental attitude. It does not believe. It knows. It never acts blindly because it can see with a superior mental insight. Faith is the reaching out attitude— an attitude that goes out upon the seeming void with the full conviction that the seeming void is the solid rock. Faith invariably breaks bounds and gives the mind a larger field of action. Then ability follows and informs the mind what to do with the new opportunity. And work completes the circle by doing what ability declares can be done. That these three factors, therefore, when properly combined will constantly acquire new worlds, constantly enlarge the possibility of achievements and constantly convert all fields of action into an ever-increasing success must therefore be evident to every mind.

Work, however, must be constructive; ability must steadily improve and faith must ever become larger and clearer. Constructive work never takes the form of drudgery, and never produces weariness, nor will such work ever do anyone any harm. No one has ever died from work, nor become sick from work. It is worry and wrong thought in general that undermines the system. So long as you get eight hours of sleep every night and live a temperate life, physically, mentally and morally, you can work every hour you are awake and enjoy it; and this is positively true when you have made your work constructive. We do not mean, however, that everybody should work steadily sixteen hours a day. It is not necessary, but if your success depends upon that amount of work in the present, do not be afraid to continue at your work every hour that you are awake. It can do you no harm, and it will be the making of a greater future for you.

Good work, constant work, constructive work, will count in every instance, and especially so when we put all there is in us into our work. Then when our work is guided by ability the results of such work will have still greater worth. And when we dwell in the attitude of faith we will constantly work up to greater and greater things.

The competent mind is the mind that is not only alive with desire for work, but that knows how to work; that can do things without being told, and that is sufficiently original to improve steadily upon the methods employed. And such a mind may be developed in anyone when the new ideas of work, ability and faith are faithfully employed. When we try to increase capacity and improve ability, we find that faith plays a part we did not suspect. It is this phase of faith that will appeal most strongly to the practical mind.

Modern psychology has discovered that the mental attitude called faith awakens new and greater forces in the mind and also increases remarkably the clearness of thought and the lucidity of intellect. The mind that lives and works in faith, as defined by the new psychology, is constantly on the verge of greater power and keener wisdom, and must therefore constantly increase in capacity and improve in ability. This is a fact that has been entirely overlooked, but it demonstrates conclusively that faith is indispensable to him who would achieve greater and greater success. However, when this remarkable value of faith is made known many minds will begin to depend almost entirely upon faith, neglecting ability and worth. But here it must be remembered that faith simply enlarges the mind, thereby producing more mental material; ability is required to employ that material properly, and work is necessary to carry out the plans and demands of ability. These three, therefore, must always combine—work, ability and faith—and when these three do properly combine great success will positively follow.

4

THE NEED OF A POWERFUL INDIVIVDUALITY.

The facts and experiences of practical life are demonstrating more fully every day that the greatest achievements come always through the strongest individualities. Therefore, in the world of action where success is the purpose, there should be a great demand for information and methods that will promote the development of individuality. And the goal of all such development should be the becoming of yourself; that is, the being of yourself so fully and so thoroughly that neither persons nor environments can exercise influences over you contrary to your own purpose and will.

It is a well-known fact that a large percentage of the failures in life come because the individual is not sufficiently himself to hold to his original purpose during trying moments. Thousands who have gone down to defeat would have won great and lasting victories if they had only held on a little longer. Then there is a very large number of failures that come because the controlling individual wavers; that IS, influenced by others to change his plans, or influenced by environment or indications to modify his original purpose.

We know that concentration upon that which are doing, as well as upon our special plans, is absolutely necessary if we are to carry things through to ultimate success of a high order. But no one can concentrate properly while he is being turned this way or that way by persons, environments, conditions or events. Those minds that have produced definite and properly constructed plans, and who can stand by those plans undisturbed until the desired results are secured, are not numerous because the development of individuality has not been promoted to any great extent.

' But as all success demands minds of this nature we realize the importance of a powerful individuality in every undertaking. And when we know that each individual is the creator of his own destiny we must naturally conclude, that that individual cannot create a great destiny who is seldom himself. You can create after your own likeness only when you are yourself. When you are under the influence of your environment you are creating a destiny just like your present environment. That is the reason why progress in the average individual has been so slow. In other words, we have created the future after the likeness of the imperfect present because we have been mostly under the influence of our present surroundings.

To see a new world of achievement patterned from something that is far superior to the present and then continue to build up that world in your own life and work—^that is one of the secrets not only in securing greater results in our present undertakings, but also in building more nobly for the future. To do this, however, we must be ourselves. We must be so strongly individualized that our own high purpose is safely protected at all times from all counteracting influences from without.

When you enter the world of action your object is to do something different, and to do your work much better than it was ever done before, because that alone can constitute real success; but you cannot do things better in the present unless you become superior to the life of the past. You cannot create something different so long as your creative powers have no other models before them than such imperfections as exist in your present environment. It is certainly evident that if we are to move forward we must give the mind a more perfect group of ideas than those that are gathered from present surroundings; but when we do secure more perfect ideas, plans or methods we cannot stand by them and see them through unless we are sufficiently strong in our own individuality to overcome such inferior influences as may surround us. In brief, we must be strong enough to be ourselves—^to stand by the best conceptions that we have formed of ourselves, and of those greater attainments and achievements that we have in view.

The man with new ideas receives very little encouragement from the public or from his associates until he has demonstrated the fact that those ideas are sound and practical. Therefore, while he is making application of his higher views, and carrying out his superior plans, he must depend upon his own strong individuality; otherwise he will fail. But this requirement has not been met by a great many in the past. Any number have appeared with original ideas, superior plans and better methods, all of which would have proved successful if thoroughly worked out; but the individuality necessary to push those things through to ultimate results was not present in every case, therefore we can remember but few in the centuries past who succeeded as fully and as greatly as it was in their power to succeed.

To originate and carry out to completion some great plan that will leave the world richer, and add to the welfare of man, that is real success; but these two essentials are not always found together in the same mind. There are many original thinkers, but they have not the individuality to carry out and push through to the end their original ideas. Then again, others have strong individual qualities and are competent to push through almost anything, but they have no originality, therefore are without the necessary material with which to work. In general, it is one mind that supplies the plans and another that carries them out, and where minds can combine in that way each one concerned will reap his share of just reward and results will be satisfactory.

In too many instances it is the one who carries out the plan who reaps the richest harvest, while the one who discovers the plan secures but a fraction of the final results. There is only a small percentage of the great inventors, discoverers and original thinkers who have received the full financial recompense due them, but no one was to blame but themselves. If they had had the originality to promote their own plans, or to stand firmly upon their own individual prerogatives, while associating with their promoters the results would have been thoroughly in their favor. Illustrations without number could be given to prove these ideas, but this will not be required, as it is clear to everybody that originality and individuality are the two great pillars in the temple of achievement, and that in order to secure the greatest results in any achievement each individual mind should possess these two prime essentials.

Where each individual mind is in possession of only one of these essentials, it will be uphill work to succeed in anything, because it requires a certain amount of individuality or push to secure the proper associates for the carrying out of wonderful ideas; and it requires a certain amount of originality to understand clearly the wonderful ideas of another . so as to work them out successfully. For this reason the proper course to pursue is to do one's very best under present circumstances and then go to work at once to develop what is lacking. Let the man who lacks individuality proceed to develop individuality to the very highest possible degree. And let the man who lacks originality learn to become an original thinker, not only in his own field of action, but in as many additional fields as possible.

Resuming our analysis of individuality and its relation to great achievements, we must not omit the fact that the most thorough use of the powers within us is possible only when we are well individualized. It requires power to do things, and the more power we possess the more we shall accomplish, provided that power is well directed. But to direct this power there must be a controlling factor in the mind; that is, the mind must be well individualized. That man who is not himself more than a part of the time does not direct his own powers at all times. When he is not strictly himself he creates in mind something that is foreign to his own purpose in life. The need of individuality, therefore, IS again most evident.

Individuality, however, cannot be developed simply through the acceptance of good advice on the subject. Such development is a science and must be studied and applied as other sciences. As individuality develops the creative forces in the mind will accumulate in that part of mentality through which your work is carried out, and will constantly increase the capacity and the efficiency of the faculties that you employ in your work. This is very important and proves conclusively why the talents of the strong individual do not give up until they have accomplished what was planned in the beginning.

Where individuality is not strong there are a number of counter tendencies in the mind, and the faculties that you employ in your vocation do not receive all the energies that are generated. Much of this energy is diverted by those counter tendencies and thus wasted. However, when individuality is well developed you are not only yourself at all times, but you naturally give your whole self to the undertaking at hand. This will cause the mind to concentrate perfectly upon those mental faculties that you employ at present, and according to a well-known metaphysical law, whenever the mind concentrates perfectly upon any faculty all the energies of the system pour into that faculty and multiply many times its capacity. That a given faculty can do better work the more power and capacity it has is a fact that anyone will understand, and that the possession of a strong individuality will enable any mind to hold all of this genius and power in the present channel of application must also be perfectly dear. We realize, therefore, the value gained by developing individuality to such an extent that every thought force produced in our systems will always be directed and applied where our work is to be done.

To create your own destiny you must be yourself at all times, and the higher your understanding of yourself the better will be the destiny that you create. To be yourself, however, does not mean that you are to imprison yourself in your own self-consciousness. There is a current idea that individualism leads to selfishness, and that the stronger your individuality becomes the more arrogant, exacting, domineering and tyrannical you become; but there is absolutely no truth to these beliefs. The strong, individualized soul is none of these things, because the stronger you become the weaker will all your faults and defects become. The well-developed individual is closer to the human race than anyone else and has a much deeper S3mipathy. Besides, it is the well-developed individual that gives the fullest and best expression to the best that is contained in human nature. When you are well individualized you will not be isolated from others, but will live more closely to the world than ever before, learning from the world as usual, but never controlled by the world. What you learn and receive you employ according to the most perfect methods, in order that greater achievements may follow.

The mind that does things worthwhile is always well rewarded. But what he does also benefits the world. So, therefore, the more you do and the more you accomplish the better off the world will be because you have lived. However, the more we study the subject the more convinced we become that individuality is an attainment we cannot afford to pass by for a moment, but the question is what to do to develop a powerful individuality.

The first step is to turn attention away from the personal self and direct thought more and more upon what is termed the great within. In this connection we must eliminate what is usually called self-consciousness; that is, being too much conscious of the visible personality. So long as we mentally dwell upon the visible side of ourselves we are conscious only of the surface. Accordingly, thought will be ordinary and feeling will be superficial. When you live, so to speak, in the shell, the outer crust, you cannot draw upon the inexhaustible resources from the within. But great minds cannot come from superficial thinking, nor from living on the surface, nor can deep or powerful thinking come from the habit of dwelling mentally upon the visible self. Therefore, if we are to become inwardly strong we must train ourselves to think better thought and live more thoroughly in the great depths of life, feeling and consciousness.

To develop individuality and to become inwardly strong mean the same, a fact that may assist many in this great work. We learn after looking closely at the subject that the lack of individuality so prevalent everywhere comes almost entirely from the race habit of superficial thinking, and such thinking continues so long as attention is directed principally upon the surface of life, thought or feeling. The turning of attention upon the depths of thought, life and feeling is absolutely necessary if we are to proceed with the development of individuality. To bring about this deeper form of thinking and to become inwardly strong so as to give thorough development to our individuality is a very simple process when we discover the real principle involved. To apply this process proceed as follows:

Take a minute or two every hour and turn all attention upon the depths of your mind. Then desire deeply and persistently to arouse the strongest energies of the great within. This is all that is necessary in the beginning. After a few days of such practice you will begin to feel yourself becoming stronger in your feelings, in your thoughts and in your convictions, and you will also begin to feel something within you that is giving you more courage, more push, more perseverance and a great deal more confidence in yourself.

As you realize these steps in advancement give credit to the new method, and you will thus find that succeeding efforts in applying this method will produce still better results. This fact is based upon the law that the more faith we have in something that is good the more good we will get out of it. As you proceed with this deeper faith you will arouse more of the latent forces, and from day to day you will realize the increase of the new power functioning more and more throughout your entire system. Then you will discover that you are getting backbone, that you are becoming absolutely fearless, and that you positively know that you can carry out your plans.

This, however, is just the beginning. You will soon become deeply interested in the new development and will give the matter more thought with more faith. What will happen henceforth will be of the greatest value to you because the development of individuality has begun. You no longer live in the shell of your being. Your mind is no longer empty or superficial. Your system is being filled up with something that has real worth and you are becoming a real power. You will discover a great change taking place throughout mind and personality. From a state of uncertainty where you did not know how to apply yourself properly, and from a state of where you did not know what the morrow would bring, you have come to a belief where you positively know how to carry out all your plans with the positive assurance of great results. From the tiny acorn that you placed in your mind a short time ago is coming the mighty oak, and from a few thoughts sown in the depths of your mind is coming those remarkable results that you have desired so long.

The beginning may be small, but perseverance in the right direction will accomplish anything. The seed from which will spring this strong individuality is the inner feeling of new power being aroused, and the simple method given above will in every case produce this inner feeling and will do so in a few days. From that foundation you can, if you persevere along the same line, build up an individuality so strong and so powerful that nothing in your life or in your environment can in any way cause you to turn to the right or to the left, or hinder your progress in any form or manner. And when you realize this you will no longer continue with the imperfect methods of the past, but will adopt all the best methods that further study along new lines will reveal to you, so that the greater results and the greater future which you now realize to be in store may be gained with a certainty.

5
THE SCIENCE OF BUSINESS SUCCESS.

Every man or woman who enters business life should succeed, and can succeed if the principles that underlie success in the commercial world are scientifically applied. There is a right way of doing things and the use of the right way must inevitably bring success. In the business world there are certain things that have to be done in order to secure results. To know what these things are and to know how to do them, in the largest and most complete sense is the secret. The majority of those who enter the business world do not succeed as well as they should and there is a reason. They do not know the requirements of business success, nor do they know how to supply those requirements. But this information everybody can secure.

To secure certain effects we must apply certain causes, and to this law there are no exceptions. There is no luck anywhere. If we want results we must do the thing that produces those results. If we want business success we must do that which produces business success, and since there are certain lines of actions that always produce success in the business world, it is evident that business can be made an exact science, a science which, when applied will produce the results desired with a certainty. Every man or woman who enters business life in any capacity whatever can succeed, and can steadily advance into greater and greater success by knowing what to do and by knowing how to do it.

In the first place the individual must place himself in the best possible working condition; that is, every factor in his system, physical or mental, that is to be employed in the work he has in view must be so directed that all its energies are given over completely to that particular work. This principle, however, has been almost wholly neglected everywhere in the business world, and for this reason the average person applies less than one-third of his power to his undertaking, the remainder is scattered and consequently lost.

The individual himself is the cause of his own success; therefore how great his success is to be will depend upon how well he applies that which is in himself. This is an idea that we have heard before, but now we must learn how to apply it. It is well enough to tell a man what he ought to do, but it is also necessary to tell him how to do it and this is the purpose of business psychology. Its value, therefore, is far greater than anyone may at first suppose.

To proceed with the placing of the entire mind in the best working condition and to establish a substantial foundation for the application of the science of business, certain lines of action will be found indispensable. To consider these briefly will therefore be necessary before proceeding further in this step.

1. Have a definite object in view, and concentrate your entire attention upon the greatest possible success which you can picture in connection with the purpose you have in mind. Think constantly of this purpose. Live for it, and desire the desired results with a desire so strong, that every atom in your being thrills with its invincible power. So long as you have no definite object in view your forces will be scattered. You will not make any real use of what is in you. You will not apply the cause of your own success. Therefore no effects can follow. To have a number of objects in view and yet be so undecided as not to give yourself to any one of them is equally detrimental. The same is true of the prevalent habit of working at one thing while wishing you had something else to do. Give the very best that is in you to what you are doing in the present and you will secure something larger and better to do in the future. This is a law that never fails. It is as exact and as universal as the law of gravitation. Proceed, therefore, to train all your forces and faculties to work for the object you have selected and be so determined to reach your goal that the force of that determination is positively irresistible.

2. Love the work you have chosen, because you can give your best only to that which you love, and great success can come only when your best— all of your best is given to your work. If you find it difficult to love your present work, think of it as a stepping stone to everything that your heart can wish for; and it is, if entered into with that faith and purpose. The most ordinary occupation can be made a channel to the greatest of deeds and the highest of attainments. Therefore, we do not have to wait for new opportunities. All that is necessary is to make the fullest use of that which is at hand now. However, the only action that is full of the best that is in us, is the action that is inspired and expressed through love, not a love for something past or future, but a love for that which we are doing now.

3. Think that you can, because he who thinks that he can will develop the power that can. When you think that you can do that which you have decided to do your mind will naturally give most of its energies to those faculties that are required in the doing of that which you have decided to do; and by giving extra life and power to those faculties they will develop, thus gaining the necessary ability to do that which you have been thinking that you can do. However, to proceed to think that you can do certain things will not at once give you the necessary ability to do those things, but that ability will immediately begin to

develop and will in time become sufficiently developed to enable you to do what you think you can do. But this thinking must not be superficial or egotistical. It must be inspired by a realization of the limitless powers that are latent within you. Think that you can with depth of feeling, a feeling that touches the very soul, and you will awaken those unbounded powers within you that can do what you think you can do. Think that you can do your present work better and you will daily develop more power and ability so that you can do it better. It is therefore possible through this law to promote continuous advancement whatever your work may be.

4. Apply your very best ability in your present work whether your recompense is sufficient or not. A great many competent men and women are underpaid, and there are several reasons, but that person who turns all his ability into his present work will soon have more opportunities for advancement than he can use. To refuse to do any more today than you are paid for today is one of the greatest obstacles to advancement and success, and there are two reasons why. In the first place, you cause a part of your ability to lie dormant which means that that ability will finally disappear, thereby diminishing your capacity and power. If you wish to develop your ability you must use all of your ability to the fullest extent. And, therefore, though you may not be paid in full for your present work, still by giving your best ability to your work you are steadily gaining in that ability so that ere long you will have the power to fill a much larger place. In the second place, by refusing to do any more than you are paid for in the present you announce to the world that you are working simply for pay. You thereby place the stamp of inferiority upon yourself, closing before you the door of progress, because when men of worth, ability and power are wanted the world will not be looking for you.

One thing is certain, however, if you apply your best you will be recompensed in the long run for all the work you do. If you do not receive it all today you will receive it later on and it will be very good when it comes. Absolute justice is the final judge in all these things and this final judgment is constantly taking place, but you will not have to work an eternity for what belongs to you. Give your best every day and the best will constantly be flowing into your own life in greater and greater abundance. In addition, by using all your ability now you will constantly develop that ability, thereby becoming a greater and a greater man. This is very important because in the attainment of a real growing success in any vocation ability is absolutely necessary, and though there are many excellent methods for the development of ability, the greater ability acquired through such methods will not become a permanent possession until it is applied in full effective use.

5. Make yourself indispensable in your present world and you will be called to occupy the highest place in that world. From that place you will soon advance to a larger world where the opportunities will be more numerous, the recompense

higher and the work more congenial. It is a fact that as soon as. you make yourself indispensable where you are, new and greater opportunities will almost immediately open before you, while, if you so live and work that your place can be refilled in one day's notice you are not in demand anywhere, and your opportunities are both few and insignificant. This being true we not only understand what it is that keeps man down, but we also understand the law through which advancement may be placed within easy reach of everybody.

6. Have the highest goal in view that you can picture in mind, and be, not only determined to reach it, but live in the strong faith that you positively will reach it. To simply aim high is not sufficient. The goal we desire to reach must be so deeply impressed upon the mind that it is a living inspiration to every thought we think. When every thought is inspired with an irresistible desire for greater things, every faculty of the mind will be kept up to the very highest point of efficiency and all the actions of the mind will work for greater things, thereby actually producing greater things. The higher the goal we have in view the greater will be the thoughts we think, provided the mind is animated with a strong, persistent desire to reach that goal. And great thoughts will invariably make a great man. To live in the strong faith that you are daily drawing nearer and nearer to your goal will not only carry you forward positively and steadily, but that faith will arouse those greater powers within you that can carry you forward. And here it is highly important to remember that it takes no more time or effort to work for great things than for small things. And he who works for great things will finally receive everything that he has worked for.

7. Create the elements of success in your own mentality by dwelling constantly in the atmosphere of success, advancement and perpetual increase. This is absolutely necessary, because the powers that make for success must exist m your own mind before you can become successful. So long as your own mind is a failure you cannot succeed in the external world because it is the mind that does things, and we do not gather figs from thistles. The mind is cause. If the effect is to be success the cause must be success; therefore all the elements of success must be created m the mind before success can be secured in the outer life of man. That is, all the actions of the mind must be made successful actions—actions that are inherently and actually constructive and that can produce results. By living in the mental atmosphere of advancement all the faculties of mind will begin to advance. The spirit of growth, attainment and achievement will animate every action and the entire mind will press on to greater things. This will make the mind more competent in every way and a competent mind is a successful mind. By living in the atmosphere of perpetual increase an accumulating process will be established in mentality. This process will increase all the powers and qualities of the mind and thus we shall have more elements that make for success. A mind that is a success in itself will produce success when practically applied in the tangible

world, because like causes produce like effects. To establish in the mind therefore the constant thought of success is absolutely necessary to him who would succeed with a certainty in the work he has undertaken.

8. Expect the best, associate with the best and desire the best with all the power of life and soul. Stand for worth and do everything in your power to become more worthy. It is quality that counts and nothing is too good for him to receive who can produce quality. Build for yourself an attractive mind and keep your personal appearance in keeping as far as possible to do so. This is extremely important because a common appearance produces a common feeling, and he who feels common will steadily and surely go down in the scale toward inferiority. Be original, try to do things better than they have ever been done before. Never follow beaten tracks, not even in details. Find a superior method. You can if you make that an aim in everything you do. It is originality that produces greatness and greatness always produces success when practically applied.

6

THE THREE-FOLD BASIS OF BUSINESS SUCCESS.

There are numbers of people in the world who believe that the door of opportunity is closed to the majority and that advancement is possible only to the lucky few. But in this they are wholly mistaken. The fact is the lucky few have made their own luck, and the many can do the same. To be numbered among the favored ones, however, an individual must be competent and must be able to make good, though these requirements are not beyond the reach of the many. Advancement is possible to all and anyone can improve himself when he knows how, and all can learn how.

The fact that the demand for competent men and women is very large everywhere and the fact that anyone may become competent places the future success of any person in his own hands. No individual therefore has anyone but himself to blame if he fails, but he can through his own individual efforts attain the greatest success that is possible to man. To attain a real and permanent success it is only a matter of understanding the principles upon which success is based and applying the laws through which practical results may be secured in one's chosen field of action. And as we are just as familiar with the principles that produce success as we are with mathematical principles there is nothing that can prevent success but the failure to apply those principles.

When these principles are systematically applied, that is, when the use of our faculties and powers is reduced to a science, the application of that science will produce success with a certainty in every individual case. The same causes produce the same effects, no matter who the person may be that applies those causes. We conclude therefore that every person who applies the science of success will positively succeed and every person can learn to apply this science. To begin, we must understand the basis of the science of business success and we find this basis to be three-fold, the first factor of which is work.

Work does things; and every stone in the temple of success is a deed well done. It is there-fare evident that the more one works the greater the success will be, provided the work is real work. And we must not forget that there is work and work, the difference between the two being very great. To work does not simply mean to use up energy. To work does not mean to tear down men while they are building up things, for the work of the man should build up the man, as well as those things that the man is building. Too much of the work done has not produced results. It has simply used up energy. The loss of this energy has made man weak and has perpetuated the belief that work is hard on the system, but it is not work that causes the physical body to wear out. The worn out condition met so frequently among men and women is caused by the using up of energy. And between real work and the mere using up of energy there is a vast difference. In fact, there is nothing whatever in common between the two.

To proceed have no fear of hard work. It will not. do you any harm, for real work does not produce weakness or weariness. On the contrary, it permanently increases the strength of the entire system. Real work generates energy just as rapidly as it consumes energy, provided the materials from which such energy is generated are supplied in abundance; and such materials may be provided through wholesome food, pure air and eight hours sleep out of every twenty-four. It is mere waste of energy, destructive or non-constructive work and strained or strenuous actions, worry and wrong thinking that cause the mind and body to wear out. But these can all be avoided; therefore, all manner of wear and tear can be completely eliminated from the human system.

The body is permeated with the mind. Every physical action is preceded by a corresponding mental action. It is therefore evident that to work properly the mind must be in the proper attitude; that is, the mind must hold itself in a certain position if all the actions of the personality are to continue in that same position. To illustrate this idea we need simply note the fact that the various faculties and forces of the person will not act in a state of harmony unless the mind holds itself in harmony during the action of those faculties and forces. In like manner, no action of the personality can be fully constructive unless the mind is in a constructive attitude at the time of that action. To state it briefly, the actions of the personality are governed by the attitudes of the mind. And since work is a series of actions, real work becomes possible only when the mind is held exclusively in those attitudes that are directly conducive to real work. This is a fact of extraordinary importance and can easily be demonstrated to be absolutely true, though anyone who is familiar with modern metaphysics will see at once that it is true. Detailed illustrations, therefore, will not be necessary in this connection.

To succeed is to move forward, and back of every forward movement there must necessarily be an abundance of good work. More work is necessary at frequent intervals if great success is to be attained, but no work ought to be hard in the sense that is wearisome or burdensome; and here we must remember that every moment of work should count. What is usually termed hard work is a full and thorough application of our energies, but such work will not be hard on the system so long as the mind is in perfect harmony with itself and its surroundings.

We may therefore enter more work with pleasure, knowing that the more we work the more we shall accomplish; and also that such work will not be wearing on the system, but will on the contrary build up the system.

To make everything count that we undertake to do, the mind should continue in a constructive attitude; that is, all work should be entered into with the deep feeling that the work will not only produce things, but will also produce greater power and capacity in the one that works. In other words, make it a point to look upon your work as a continuous cause of physical and mental development and you will not only build up greater and greater success, but such work will also build up your system. Enter your work in this attitude and it will not only make your business a success, but it will make you a success. It will produce a fine man as well as a fine income.

Ability gives worth to things; and real success means the perpetual increase of worth, not only in the man's product but in the man himself. The greater the worth of the product, the greater the price that may he secured as the world wants good things and is willing to pay well to get them; but it is only the mind of ability that can produce good things. Work alone will do things, but the value of those things will depend upon how much ability was applied in the work. It is not a number of ordinary things that constitutes success. Success is the power to produce the extraordinary both in quality and in quantity. And success comes only through the practical application of a mind that is large as well as superior. However, those who do not have such a mind at the present time need not think that success is not in store for them, for ability can be developed even to a remarkable degree; though the first essential is to use thoroughly what ability we already possess.

To work successfully all work must be constructive to the highest possible degree, but it requires ability to so direct one's efforts that every action will do something worthwhile. The mind that lacks ability misdirects the majority of its actions; those actions therefore produce nothing while those actions that can be properly directed, usually fail to produce quality, for the fact is that no action can produce anything of real value unless there is ability in that action. And since success comes only through the production of good things ability becomes indispensable to him who would succeed in the best sense of that term.

To develop your business ability make the fullest use of what ability you now possess and devote as much time as convenient to the further development of that ability. Use your talents now, fully and thoroughly, whether you receive a high salary or not. If you are waiting to use your best talents until you receive a high salary you will never receive such a salary, and your talents will continue to lie dormant. By making the fullest use of the ability you now possess, you not only develop your ability by bringing out the best that is in you, but you prove to those who know you, that you are fully able to fill a larger place; and since competent men and women are in great demand everywhere, you will soon find a larger place waiting for you.

Demonstrate by your work, not by your words, that you are competent and you will have more opportunities for advancement than you can use. If you are in business for yourself the same law will hold without any exceptions whatever. The world wants good things. Therefore, produce them and let the world know what you can produce. You will soon find that your establishment will need enlargement. The world goes where they receive the best service. Supply that service therefore, by making the fullest and best use of your ability. You will find business in, abundance positively coming your way.

The development of business ability is a subject that should receive most thorough attention and since scientific methods through which this ability can be developed have been discovered, every moment we give to this matter will positively count. Accordingly, those who are not competent, and who have heretofore been unsuccessful, need not be discouraged. It is just as natural to develop ability along any line as it is to develop muscle.

In addition to the full use of your present ability the mind should be kept in that attitude that is most conducive to the growth of the mind while present ability is being exercised. It is a fact that the proper application of ability will develop that ability during working hours just as the proper use of muscle will increase the size and power of that muscle. To exercise your ability m the proper mental attitude look upon your present work as a means to advancement. Constantly think of your work in this way and impress this thought so deeply upon your mind that whenever you think of your work you think of advancement. Through this attitude you will relate yourself to your work in such a way that everything you do will be used directly in promoting your own success; and what is just as important, when you think of your present work as a means to advancement you animate your work with the spirit of advancement. This will not only push your work, but it will cause you to do far better work, and better work invariably means advancement both in yourself and in your sphere of action.

Faith works up to greater things; and since real success means higher attainments and greater achievements faith becomes absolutely necessary to a truly successful life. It is the truth that no one ever pressed on to greater things without some degree of faith, and it is also the truth that the greatest men have had the largest faith. Faith as employed here, however, is not a belief about something. It is a mental attitude—^the reaching out attitude. Faith is that something in man that is constantly breaking bounds, that is ever on the verge of greater things, that is .ever working up toward the larger and the greater, and that knows through an interior insight how to use in the present those greater possibilities that are being discerned as the mind looks out toward the future.

To be successful to a great degree you must be far sighted; that is, you must have that insight that knows how to do the right thing at the right time, and this insight is produced by the attitude of faith. When you have faith in the greater, your mind will constantly enter into the life and the power of the greater and will consequently gain possession of the greater. It is therefore simple to understand that the mind that works in the attitude of faith must unfailingly work up to greater things.

Faith will increase the clearness of the thought and the brilliancy of the mind because faith takes consciousness into the upper story of the mind where superior intelligence actually does exist. Faith awakens the higher and the mightier forces within us, and expands consciousness in every direction; the mind is thereby enlarged, mental capacity is increased and the essentials to greater ability supplied. Faith brings out the best that one may possess now The man who has faith in himself therefore will be his best at all times. He will do his best no matter what his occupation may be and he who does his best in his present work will invariably be promoted to a work that is better.

The man who has faith in his work will secure the best results from that work. Accordingly, he will pave the way for a greater enterprise; and by having faith in everything and everybody he will dwell mentally with the best that there is in life. This is extremely important because it is the mind that constantly concentrates upon the better and the greater, that will constantly work up to the greater and the better:

From the foregoing it will be clearly evident to all that the three-fold basis of a business science will necessarily be composed of these three factors— work, ability and faith.

7

THE SEVEN FACTORS IN BUSINESS SUCCESS.

It has been frequently stated, and wisely, that when the man is made right his work will take care of itself, but the problem with the average person is, how to proceed to make himself right. He may realize that his inability to accomplish as much as he has in mind is due entirely to his own shortcomings, but he does not always know what those shortcomings happen to be; and even though he should know, the question is where to begin to mend after some definite idea has been gained as to what constitutes the law of successful achievement.

Every person knows that self-improvement is the only key to success, but the nature of self-improvement is not clearly understood, and definite methods through which self-improvement may be promoted have not been worked out to a satisfactory degree. The reason why, however, can easily be traced to the fact that the psychology of life, thought and action has heretofore been given but little attention.

When the relationship that naturally exists between the man and his work is closely examined, we find that there are three great essentials to the most thorough expression of the man in his work, and these three are power, ability and originality. When we search for those elements that make man what he is, and that could, through greater development make him more than he is, we find the secret to be personality, character and soul. The man who desires to become more than he is, therefore, and who desires to promote real self-improvement must develop personality, character and soul, while the man who desires to make the best practical use of what he already is must develop power, ability and originality. When these six great factors are thoroughly developed and practically applied through the seventh great factor—system—success must inevitably follow.

To develop personality the man should be trained to think with every nerve and fibre in the entire human system. Every thought should be felt and deeply felt in every atom of one's being. And when this feeling is held in a poised, positive attitude personal growth and power will invariably develop. It is a well-known fact that the strong, well poised personality is always selected for the best places in life because such a personality always produces the best impression. Such a personality always carries the stamp of quality and worth, therefore finds little difficulty in forging to the front.

In the commercial world few things are more important than confidence; and there is nothing that inspires confidence so quickly and so completely as a well-developed personality.

The strong personality feels deeply, is conscious of a great deal of life and power, but this power is always held in poise, and it is much power held in perfect poise that makes the personality what we wish it to be.

The development of character in connection with commercial success has been almost wholly ignored, but the fact is that every person who desires to make the most of himself simply must give character the most thorough development possible. Character is the power that directs all the forces and faculties in their constructive actions. It is character that keeps everything in what may be termed the straight or correct line of action. And it is such actions that produce the greatest results Character prevents the scattering of forces and the misdirection of forces; therefore the more character a person has the fewer will be his mistakes, and the more numerous will be those actions that count for something.

That element of life that we speak of as soul, is that finer something in the nature of man that gives superiority to everything through which it may be expressed. And since self-improvement implies the increase of superiority it is evident that the cause of superiority, that is, soul, becomes indispensable. No person can become superior or develop superiority in any of his talents unless he unfolds that finer something that is called soul whether the unfoldment be conscious or unconscious, though it is the conscious unfoldment and development that counts. The unconscious is always limited and is never certain.

To develop soul the first essential is to realize the meaning of soul and then try to feel the element of soul in every thought and action. To train consciousness to enter more deeply into the finer elements of worth, quality and superiority will aid remarkably in producing this finer feeling of soul, and when one begins to feel soul the constant unfoldment of more and more soul can be promoted with comparative ease.

No person should ever think of himself as inferior or as a mere limited human entity. On the contrary, every thought should be stamped with the realization of that superiority that does exist in the depth of real life, and every action of mind should aspire toward the acquisition of greater worth for every faculty, talent or power that may exist in one's being.

To think constantly of soul will increase the expression of soul, provided one thinks of soul as being the cause of quality and worth. But the right understanding of soul must be given in every thought or that thought will not convey the quality of expression desired. There is no power in the human mind that can promote development along any line as thoroughly as that of direct thinking. But in the average mind thinking is neither direct nor designed. Most thoughts are not animated by any purpose or any degree of quality, therefore convey no particular effect upon the mind. To employ this principle of direct thinking we should animate every thought with a thorough understanding of the quality that we desire to develop and we shall find that every thought we think will tend to develop the quality desired. To develop soul, therefore, the principle is to animate every thought with a deep and thorough understanding of soul, and then to give the feeling of soul to every thought. The result will be that every thought you think will give more soul to you.

The constant and harmonious development of personality, character and soul will promote a self-improvement that actually is improvement. The individual will not only become right, but will become more, and he who becomes more will accomplish more. In the practical application of the personality, the character and the soul that one may possess, the first essential is power, both mental power and personal power. It is power that does things. It is power that makes the ideal real. And it is power that causes our best ideas to become tangible achievements. Therefore to turn the best that is in us to practical account more power must be developed.

To increase one's power the first essential is to prevent the waste of the power already generated in the system. This is accomplished first through poise, and second through the constructive use of all the energies in the system. The principle is to turn every force into some building process. Even physical pleasures should be animated with the desire for attainment, and the forces employed in those pleasures will promote the development of one or more factors in the human system.

The second essential to the increase of power is to impress the desire for more power upon the subconscious side of every atom in one's being. It is the truth that every part of mind and body does contain more power in the potential state. More energy is latent everywhere in the human system than we have ever used or even dreamed of, and all of this energy can be brought out for practical use. To bring out this energy concentrate attention upon every part of the system and make that concentration deeply felt and strong. Impress upon every part of your personality all the power you are conscious of now, and you will thereby arouse the greater power that is latent within you. This method if practiced in conjunction with perfect poise will in a short time largely increase the power and capacity of the mind. And if practiced continuously there is practically no limit to the working capacity that may be secured thereby.

There are many methods for the development of ability that might be jDresented, but the simplest and most effective is that of the direct power of thought. To apply this method form in the mind as clear an understanding as possible of the real nature of that ability that you wish to develop. Then try to realize through mind picturing the nature of that ability and stamp that picture upon every action of mind. In other words, so think that every thought you think will be created in the exact likeness of the ability you wish to develop. Every thought has creative power, but that power will always create after the likeness of the thought itself. Therefore when every thought you think is an exact image of the faculty you wish to develop, the creative power of every thought will tend to produce or develop that ability. In the average mind, however, this creative power is almost entirely wasted because no thought is given a definite purpose. What one group of thoughts may build up another will tear down, while the majority of the thoughts we think do nothing but scatter their energies the moment they are produced.

When the mind is trained to think always of the most perfect understanding that can be formed of the ability that is to be developed, every thought that is produced will give its creative power to the building up of that ability. And as there will under such conditions be no thoughts to interfere with the building process it can readily be understood that such a method can develop ability even to a remarkable degree.

The development of originality depends upon the practical use of what may be gained from the imagination. To try to formulate practical plans, methods and systems from the many ideas that are constantly presented by the imagination is to continue the development of originality. To apply this principle the products of the imagination should be arranged and rearranged again and again until something practical is evolved, or until original ideas, plans and methods are produced in connection with one's line of work. And in this connection it is well to remember that the more attention we give to the practice of becoming more and more original, the more power and activity we give to the faculty of originality itself. In other words, we develop more and more originality the more we try to be original in all things.

After all the essentials in the building of mind, and the practical application of what is in mind have been provided, there is still another factor that may be added to the seven already mentioned; and this is nothing more or less than interior insight. It is not a separate factor however, in every case as it is more or less combined with several of the other factors mentioned; but it is a faculty that should be highly developed in every case, as it is this faculty that enables the mind to know how to do the right thing at the right time.

It is interior insight that gives foresight, that makes the man long-headed, so to speak, and that enables the mind to discern real opportunities whenever they appear. There are some minds that intuitively know genuine opportunities when they see them. Other minds almost invariably choose circumstances that have no possibilities whatever; and the difference lies in the development of interior insight. There never was a successful man who did not possess this insight to a great degree, whether he was aware of it or not. And there never was a great enterprise that was not engineered more or less by this faculty. Men and women who claim to be very practical may overlook this fact, or may call this insight by some other name, but it is the same insight nevertheless, and no great success is possible without it.

To develop this faculty make it a practice to use your insight, or at any rate to try to use it whenever information of any kind is desired; and train the mind to expect first-hand information from this source on every subject. Do not permit the imagination to become too active, however, while this faculty is being employed because the clearest fact is discerned when the mind is acting in the upper story. A high and orderly development of this faculty will be found to be a rare achievement, and every mind that aims at greater things should give this matter not only thorough attention, but all the time that may be required

8

THE USE OF THE MIND IN PRACTICAL ACHIEVEMENT.

Whatever our views of metaphysics may be, materialistic or idealistic, we all realize that it is the use of the mind that determines results in every undertaking. Back of muscle and brain there is mind, and how much the muscles and brains are to accomplish will depend upon how they are used, directed and applied by the mind. The mind is not only the power that controls and directs every action in mentality or personality, but the mind also determines the efficiency of every action.

It is therefore evident that an ignorant use of the mind will cause every action to be a perverted action, a detrimental action or an unsuccessful action, while the intelligent use of the mind will cause every action to produce with a certainty the very results that were originally intended. If an effort fails the cause may invariably be traced to the wrong use of the mind in the direction of that effort. No effort can possibly fail that is properly applied at the right time and place. This is certainly a self-evident fact, and since it is the mind that must make the application, the intelligent use of the mind becomes the one important factor in determining results, be the work purely physical, purely mental, or a blending of the two.

To train the mind to direct properly the various actions of the mentality or the personality, all the forces of mind should be concentrated continuously upon the purpose that is held in view. This will draw all the energies of the mind together into the working line, and as every action is produced by some form of energy it is evident that if all the energies are moving toward the object in view every action will work toward that object. Under such circumstances all the power of mind and body will be turned into the work that is being promoted and as all this power will have to pass through those faculties that are directly employed in that work, those faculties will steadily develop in ability and capacity. This will make you more competent than you ever were before, and the competent mind simply must succeed.

To concentrate all the energy of the mind upon a certain faculty is to develop that faculty. This has been demonstrated conclusively, but when that energy is practically applied in some constructive work while it is accumulating in that faculty, the development will be more rapid and the increased capacity will be permanent. This is what takes place when the mind turns all of its power upon the work it is doing now. Therefore, to use the mind in this way is to make present action directly instrumental in promoting further promotion. Through this law the doing of little things can prepare us for the doing of great things, and invariably will if all the power of mind is focused upon the work of the present moment.

The principal reason why the average person does not advance as he should is found in the fact that he gives only as much of his mental power to his work as may be necessary to do it fairly well. The rest of his power is scattered and wasted through aimless thinking, purposeless imagination, and a dividing and a subdividing of attention. Your present work is the motor-car that is to carry you forward. If you turn your power into the motor you will move forward rapidly, but if the greater part of your power is scattered your progress will t: slow. But it is the mind that directs or misdirects the power that is being generated in the human system. Therefore, whether all the power is to be well directed or not depends upon the use of the mind.

To concentrate the whole of attention upon the purpose that is being promoted becomes an easy matter through steady practice along this line, though it will become easier still if the most interesting viewpoint of this purpose is gained at the outset. We naturally concentrate all of our power upon that in which we are deeply interested, and we can find an interesting viewpoint in everything if we look for it While we are looking for this interesting viewpoint the mind will unconsciously or subconsciously become interested in the subject Accordingly, we will proceed to concentrate without trying, and that is the best concentration of all.

To dwell mentally upon the idea of success or to keep the greatest imaginable success constantly in view, and to picture oneself upon the path of perpetual increase, these are matters of great importance. To think constantly of perpetual increase is to promote perpetual increase in your own ability and power, provided you are using thoroughly what ability and power you now possess. This is a great law, so great that it merits the constant attention of every aspiring mind. Through this law unlimited success is placed within reach of every person who really wants success, because the perpetual increase of ability and power will, if applied, produce a perpetual increase in attainment, achievement and tangible possessions.

To dwell mentally upon the idea of success and upon the life of success, is to produce the life and the power and the understanding of success in the mind itself. Such a mind will know success, what 16 conducive to success, and will have the power to push its ideas into successful action. To dwell mentally upon success will also train the mind to use its own faculties more successfully, and it will train those faculties to formulate successful plans methods, and such systems of application as make for success.

To know what to do with present opportunities is one of the great essentials to attainment and achievement and the mind that dwells constantly in the very life and thought of success will develop that finer judgment that knows the successful side of everything. Such a mind can discern what is practical, and what is not, in every circumstance or possibility that may be considered, because being filled with the very spirit of success, it knows what has success in it and what has not. The mind that can discover successful plans and that knows how to apply them will positively succeed no matter what the circumstances may be. And to think success, work for success, and press on toward greater and greater success, is to open the mind to new methods for promoting success, and new systems for enlarging the range of one's individual success. Success, therefore, in fact, greater and greater success must follow with a certainty.

The mind should see only the successful side of everything, that is, the bright side, the rich side, the growing side, the side of new opportunities and the side of greater possibilities. This attitude of mind will keep all the faculties in the best working condition. The entire mind will be kept at the high water mark of ability, capacity and efficiency; confidence in one's self, in one's associates and in one's work will be complete; faith, that great essential to success will be high and strong, and a most excellent impression will be produced upon all minds with whom we may come in contact. The mind that lives in the upper story, so to speak, not only displays all its faculties and talents to the best advantage, but actually employs all its forces to the best advantage. Such a mind not only makes good now, but impresses everybody with the fact that it can do more just as soon as the opportunity is supplied; and the desired opportunity will not be withheld very long from such a mind.

To complain at any time or under any circumstances is a misuse of the mind. It causes the mind to fall down to its worst. To permit the mind to think of failure or impending trouble is to go down mentally into conditions of failure and trouble. This will cause the mind to become troubled, disturbed, and confused, and such a mind will make any number of mistakes, do nearly everything wrong and be its worst in nearly every sense of the term. To permit hard-luck thought of any description, or to listen to talk of that sort, will produce the same results; the mind will be taken down, and for the time being will become weak and incompetent.

To overcome these tendencies resolve to create your own good luck. Know that you can because it is true that you can. Then eliminate completely every thought, error or suggestion that implies anything to the contrary. The tendency to complain, or to expect hard luck, will almost invariably impress other minds with the belief that you are incompetent; in brief, that you are a failure or that there is something wrong with you. Successful minds, therefore, will have nothing to do with you, and instead of securing the best places in the commercial world you will have to go down and accept something that is ordinary or inferior.

The habit of complaining, or taking the dark view whenever anything goes wrong, will also impress your own mind with failure, and with the belief that you are incompetent. After a while you will begin to think that you do not amount to much, and when such thought begins to take possession of your mind you will soon be counted among those who have failed. If you wish to do greater and greater things you must think that you can, because when you think that you can, you develop the power that can. Thus in the course of time you will actually be able to do the very things that you thought you could do; so therefore it is safe to "hitch your wagon to a star."

To train your mind to work in perfect harmony with the elements and forces of success, try as far as possible to associate only with people who are successful or people who want success, who talk only success and who are living personifications of the very atmosphere of success.

Every mental state should be a working power toward greater things and should be animated with the life that has within it the possibilities of greater things. No mental state therefore should be permitted that contemplates the lesser, that drifts toward the lesser, or that has the tendency to be satisfied to work only for the lesser. All thinking should be animated with the spirit of attainment and achievement, and every thought should deeply feel, and persistently feel, the desire to work with all its life and power for the very highest success you have in view.

Stand for the highest worth. Aim to realize greater and greater worth and daily impress upon every part of your mind the highest conception of quality and worth that you can possibly picture. This will develop superiority in every phase of mentality, and the result will be that superior mental power, superior talents and superior ability will inevitably follow. The mind that develops greater worth will gain the ability to produce things that have greater worth. The man with such a mind, therefore, will be worth more in the commercial world, his labor and his brains will command a higher price and his products will be in great demand. By increasing his own mental and personal worth he will increase the worth and the value of his work because the man himself is the cause, his work is the natural effect

The inferior mind cannot expect to produce high priced products, nor can extraordinary achievements proceed from ordinary talents. He who would do the greater, therefore, must first, become greater; and he can become greater by giving his best ability to his present work and by using his-present work through which to express all the worth, all the quality, all the capacity and all the power that he may now possess. In other words, by training his whole mind to apply itself thoroughly to everything he may undertake to do he will develop the whole mind. This will produce the greater mind, and the greater mind will soon have the privilege to do the greater things.

Another essential in turning the whole of the mind and the best there is in the mind into the efforts of today, is to be deeply interested in what you are doing today, and to have a deeply felt love or admiration for that work. This is not sentiment, but an exact scientific principle. The man who works simply for the wages he is to get will always get small wages because such a mind will not improve. In like manner, the man who remains satisfied with a small business, just enough to give him a living, will always continue in a small business, and his living will be cheap and ordinary. The fact is that such people do not turn all the powers of their mind into their work. They simply use enough mind to keep things a-going; the rest of their powers are wasted.

Make it a point, therefore, when you accept a position, or enter any kind of business, to love it; love it with all the heart and soul that you can arouse; and you will find this an easy matter when you know that your present work is the path to those greater things that your heart may wish for. When you deeply love your work you will naturally concentrate your whole mind upon your work, and you will use all your power in your work. This means better work and a more rapid development of your own ability and talent.

It is the truth that he who loves what he is doing today will be given something better to do tomorrow. He who gives his whole heart and his whole mind to little things will soon have the capacity to take charge of greater things, and he will also have the opportunity. To state it briefly, when you concentrate all your mental and personal power upon your present purpose you will accomplish that purpose because no one can fail who applies his whole mind to his work; and to use the whole mind constantly in everything we do is to develop the whole mind more and more. This means a greater and a greater mind to be followed invariably by still greater success.

9

PRACTICAL RULES IN BUSINESS PSYCHOLOGY.

1. Have something to give to the world that is worth giving; something that the world wants. Your success depends not only upon your own efforts, but also upon the degree of appreciation that those efforts may have the power to call forth. No matter how good your work may be if it is not appreciated, results will be limited. You will be wasting a large portion of your time and you will benefit no one, not even yourself. To secure appreciation your object must be, not to give that which you think the world ought to want, but to give that which you know the world does want. Make it a point to please others and you will also please yourself. Thousands of brilliant minds fail entirely because they imagine their talents will be degraded if brought down to the wants of the world, but no talent will be brought down so long as it is used in promoting the welfare of others, no matter whether those others be cultured or not. Give your talents and your ability to those who need them, and make your efforts so simple that the largest number possible can appreciate what you are trying to do. Give the largest number what they need and what they want, and make what you give so worthy that everybody will want to take advantage of your service without being persuaded to do so.

2. Be determined to serve the world better in your line than it was ever served before. Whatever you do, know that it can be done better, and know that that better can be done by you. The fact that others have failed must not influence your mind or your conduct in the least. We are not in bondage to the shortcomings of others, nor the failures of the past. What we are determined to do we can do because we have the power. In this connection we must remember that there is no success that is greater than perpetual advancement in one's own ability to do the greater and the better, and there is nothing that gives more contentment or joy. To make the better one's goal and to cause all the energies of being, to work for that goal, is to enter the pathway to real success—the success that is success, and that perpetually reproduces itself in greater and greater success. To be determined to serve the world better than it was ever served before is to improve one's self and one's work in one's present vocation which will ere long open the way to a far more important vocation. He who is positively determined to do the best will positively have the opportunity to do the best.

3. Know that you can do what you want to do because there is no limit to the power that is latent

within you. The greatest obstacle to higher attainments and greater achievements is the belief that the power we possess is limited and that the ability we possess is as large now as it ever will be. This obstacle, therefore, must be removed through the realization of the truth in this matter. The truth is that every form of ability can be developed indefinitely and that the powers of mind and soul are inexhaustible. To live in the perfect realization of that truth and to animate every thought and desire with the very spirit of that truth is to promote the development of every form of ability that we may be using now, and also to enlarge perpetually the capacity of mind so that a larger and a larger measure of power will be unfolded, perpetuated and expressed. When you inwardly know that you can do what you want to do, you place yourself in conscious possession of the power that can do what you want to do; and this knowing will steadily grow in mind as every thought is created more and more in the likeness of the truth just mentioned.

4. You will not go down so long as you do not permit your mind to go down. One of the great secrets of success is to keep the mind up even though everything else may seem to go down. If the mind persists in staying up, things will soon change and begin to come up again. This is a law that never fails, and if it was thoroughly applied under every circumstance it would prevent practically every failure in the world. The mind is the master, provided its mastership is exercised; and the way the mind goes everything else will go also. Things will follow very soon, if not at once, provided the mind holds fast to its high ideals and falters not. The mind that dwells constantly upon the bright sides will soon cause all things to leave the world of darkness and begin to create brightness. The mind that aims perpetually to realize higher attainments and greater achievements will cause all things to work together for the promotion of such attainments and achievements. The mind that continues in absolute faith even though every external indication points to certain failure—that mind will cause all things to change in their courses, to cease working for failure and to proceed to produce those very things that the mind believed with faith that it could secure. Permit nothing, therefore, to take the mind down, because if the mind persists in staying up, things will positively take a turn and come up also. Thus the threatening failure will terminate in a still greater success.

5. Know that your life is in your own hands; that you may therefore do with your life whatever you wish to have done. All power comes from life. To increase the expression of life is to increase the expression of everything that has real worth. And in him who has taken the expression of life into his own hands, the expression of life may be increased in any measure desired. When you know that

your life is in your own hands you will begin to live the way you want to live, and the energies of your being will begin to work together for the promotion of that which you wish to have promoted; the scattering of forces will cease and all things will move toward the goal you have in view. But so long as your life is not in your own hands it will be more or less in the hands of environment. You will not live, therefore, for your own welfare and advancement, but you will live for every passing idea or notion that the shifting of circumstances may suggest. Real success, however, will be impossible in such a life, because to succeed in any achievement you must live for that achievement. But before you can live for anything definite you must realize that your life is in your own hands, and that you can live for anything by positively deciding to do so. Strictly speaking, it is not necessary to take your life into your own hands, it already is in your own hands. What is necessary is to cease giving it away to every whim or circumstance that may be passing by. Your life is your own. Keep it for yourself, therefore, because it was given to you to be used by you, and by you alone. Nothing else can use your life. Accordingly, when you scatter your life abroad you deprive yourself of that which no one else can use. To apply the truth in this idea, live constantly m the realization of the great truth that your life is your own and that you can turn all of its power into any channel that you may select. Then select the path that leads to real success. Live in that path with all your life, and the goal you have in view will positively be reached.

6. Begin where you are. Do perfectly what you are doing now, but keep the mind open constantly for greater powers and greater opportunities. To dream too much of the future is to neglect the present. And to be indifferent to the lesser while yearning for the greater is to continue to live in the lesser. Be ambitious, be determined to rise in the scale, but use all the force of that determination in perfecting and enlarging the sphere of the present moment. Make the present moment a great cause by turning all your power into the work of the present moment, and from that great cause will come great effects in the coming days. Every vocation, every environment and every circumstance contain possibilities that we may never have known. To work out these greater possibilities is to make the present moment a great beginning of a far greater future, but we cannot enter into the conscious possession of the hidden possibilities that the present moment may contain so long as we give our deep thought to the future and our superficial thought to the present. There is only one place to begin, and that is where we are living and working now. There is only one possibility upon which we can concentrate with success, and that is the possibility that the p-resent moment holds in store.

7. Have great objects in view, but keep them secret. We give our greatest powers to those things that we think of as too sacred to mention. Never speak generally about those things that you wish to accomplish, unless it should be to

those who are in perfect harmony with your ideas and plans. And under no circumstances should we speak of our higher ambitions unless the mind be in the upper story at the time. To speak or think of the great things we have in view while the mind is in ordinary or superficial states is to give a measure of inferiority to those things which may lessen results or even produce failure. Before those greater things are given thought, the mind should be elevated to the highest and most sacred places within, that consciousness can possibly realize, because while we are in those loftier states of thought we give immense power to that of which we may be thinking at the time. This is a law of extraordinary importance, and may be applied with remarkable results in any sphere of action. To think of your plans while in ordinary states of mind is to give only ordinary thought to those plans, and nothing can succeed that is not animated by something better than by mere ordinary thought. The same is true when we are doing something of exceptional value. It will be a failure unless we think of it all as being too lofty and too important to be dealt with except in the very highest and strongest states of mind. The higher the action of mmd the greater the power of mind. And the more sacred the thought the higher the action of that thought. This is the law, and to those who have great and worthy objects in view this law is positively indispensable.

8. Dwell mentally with the superior, the marvelous and the limitless. Superficial consciousness and every phase of superficial thinking must be entirely avoided or the development of ability will be retarded. Success depends not only upon ability, but upon the constant improvement of ability. And the more closely the mind is brought in touch with the elements of quality and superiority the more rapidly will every faculty develop. To dwell mentally with the superior is to unfold superiority. To dwell mentally with the marvelous is to develop the imagination, the power of originality and to inspire the mind with those ascending tendencies that invariably lead to greatness. And to dwell mentally with the limitless is to place the mind in that position where it can constantly draw upon that power that is limitless. Success, therefore, and great success, must invariably follow.

9. Believe in justice. Establish yourself firmly upon the principle of absolute justice and an exact equivalent, and you will receive what you deserve. Never desire to get something for nothing, as such a desire will decrease your own capacity by retarding the expression of yourself. When you desire to get something for nothing you desire to give nothing in return. You thereby hold back a part of your own ability, which means retarded growth. Have absolute faith in justice and you will secure justice from everybody and under every circumstance. This is a law that cannot fail, for even though it may not prove itself at once, it finally will in every instance bring to every individual what actually belongs to that individual.

10. Your own will come to you provided you live absolutely upon the principle of the exact equivalent, but your own will be only as great as yourself. Therefore, if you wish to increase the quality and the quantity of that which is coming into your life, you must first increase the worth and the power of your own life. By becoming larger than you are you will receive more than you do. Things that are worthwhile will accumulate in your world in proportion to your ability to do that which is worthwhile; that is, when that ability is thoroughly and constantly applied.

11. Real success implies the advancement of the individual himself and the advancement of the world in which the individual may live. It means the building of a greater man and the promotion of greater achievements in the environments of that man. Real success does not simply mean the accumulation of things, but in the development of a personality so strong and so great that it must invariably attract great things, and as many great things as may be necessary to promote the largest and the richest state of existence possible. In the promotion of real success there must be two leading objects in view. The first must be to make yourself greater than you are, and this object must always come first. You are the cause of your own success. Therefore, the greater you are the greater will be your success, because a great cause will invariably produce a great effect. The second object must be to promote higher attainments and greater achievements, and this will naturally be fulfilled when the growing mind is constantly expressed in constructive thought and effective action. The idea is to become much and you will do much; and he who does much will receive much because like invariably attracts like. Causes and effects are always similar and the law works both ways. The very same law that brings disaster will, if reversed, bring us everything that the heart may desire.

12. Air castles are indispensable^ but they must be built upon a foundation composed wholly of your own worth. The only air castles that fall are the ones that have nothing but dreams upon which to stand. The man who is positively determined to do what he aims to do, and who will not only give his whole life, but the best that is contained in his life, to the purpose he has in view, may build any number of air castles. They will all stand the test of life, and he will have the pleasure to really dwell in them all in days that are soon to be. He who is determined to make good will shortly have the power to make anything. His ambitions, therefore, cannot be too lofty nor too strong; neither can his castles in the air be too gorgeous. All his dreams will come true because he does not only dream dreams, but actually goes to work and makes those dreams come true. The principle, therefore, is to hitch your wagon to a star; but be sure that the chain is strong. Thus you will scale the heights and there will be no fall.

13. Everything you do will count. Nothing is lost, but whether it is to work for you, or against you, will depend upon what you were working for, when the thing in question was created. However, those adverse forces that are lurking in the mistakes of the past may be transmuted and may be directed to work just as faithfully for you as they previously worked against you. He who is positively determined to do what he is ambitious to do can change everything in his favor, though this determination must be animated with a ceaseless and persistent desire for the realization of the goal in view; and must be literally alive with the spirit of that faith that is faith.

14. Become a strong, positive center in your own world, and constantly improve upon the worth of that center. The law of attraction is the basis •f all real success; therefore, the greater the center of attraction which is you, yourself, the greater will be those things that will naturally gravitate into your world. You cannot naturally take what belongs to others, for you can attract only what belongs to yourself, and that alone can belong to you that is an exact equivalent of what you are and what you have done. To become a positive center in your own world harmonize all the elements and forces in your own being by constantly feeling the harmony that exists within you in the real principle of harmony. Develop poise and train all the energies of your mind and body to move towards the limitless within. Realize that you can draw upon the forces that exist all about you and feel the constant accumulation of those forces in your entire system. Through this process you will awaken the greater powers within you and you will thus attract the finer forces from without. You will therefore become a center of great power both in mind and personality; and much does attract more.

15. Being and doing must be the objects in view. To live a great life in the midst of great attainments and great achievements—^that is real success. And the beginning of such a success can be made now by using, according to the science of success, every opportunity that may be at hand now. He who makes the best use of what is at hand now will soon have the opportunity to use something better; and since this process may be perpetuated indefinitely there is no end to the greatness of success that is real success. The fundamental principle in the science of real success is the building of greatness in mind and the use of that greatness in the building of the better, the higher and the superior in the world of man, both in the physical world and in the mental world.

10

THE NEW WAY OF DOING THINGS.

The world admires the man who does things, and therefore imitates as much as possible his type of thought and action. But to try to do what another is doing will not be productive of results unless the same ability and capacity is secured. Mere external imitation, therefore, is useless; but internal imitation may prove highly profitable, and such an imitation tends to develop the ability and the capacity required. He who would do things worthwhile must develop the power that can do those things, and to develop that power he must do things in the within before he attempts to do things in the without. The doing of things in the within, however, has been almost wholly neglected in our ceaseless endeavor to secure immediate results in the tangible world. And for this reason tangible results that are really worthy have not been as numerous as we should like, while shallow minds have been too numerous.

A fact of importance to consider in this connection is this, that when we concentrate the whole of attention upon the doing of things that can be seen we cause the mind to dwell more and more on the surface until all mental action becomes superficial; and when this condition appears there will not be sufficient depth nor power in the mind to do the things worthwhile. This same condition will appear more or less in the mind of the person whose sole desire is to be practical; that is, he will in time wing the mind so completely out into the objective that consciousness will come out away from everything in mentality that has richness, quality and worth.

When the mind gives the whole of attention to external things it will necessarily fail to give sufficient thought to those inner qualities of mentality that alone can deal intelligently with things. Such a mind therefore will try to do things without possessing the knowledge and the power that can do things. There is such a thing as becoming so completely absorbed in your purpose that you forget to provide yourself with those essentials that alone can fulfill that purpose. In other words, you become so carried away with your desire to overcome the enemy that you forget your ammunition. Nothing worthwhile can be accomplished without mental capacity, and every mode of mental action that tends to keep the mind at work on the surface alone will cause the mind to become shallow.

The mind that can do things is the mind that is trying to do things both in the within and in the without. By acting upon the internal phases and elements of mentality, capacity and power are developed; and by acting upon tangible things that capacity and power are turned to practical use. When this new method of doing things, that is, acting both in the inner and in the outer worlds is continued, the development of mental capacity as well as practical ability will be steadily promoted. Such a mind, therefore, will not only do things, but will constantly do better things and greater things. That man, however, who neglects to do things in the within while using what power and capacity he may possess in the doing of things in the without will gradually diminish that power and capacity, and his work will accordingly decrease in value. His practical ability will exhaust itself because he has failed to renew and develop the power of that ability; but this failure is found in the great majority. Therefore, instead of the added years bringing added power, increased ability and greater efficiency, the reverse is nearly always the case. Instead of moving forward with the years, the average man gradually deteriorates in mind and efficiency. And the reason why, is found in the fact that the constant development of the great within is neglected.

The man who gives his whole attention to the accumulation of wealth may gain wealth for a while if he originally possessed accumulative ability; but the ceaseless concentration of the mind upon mere things will in the long run cause the inner mentality to become barren, and there will be no further increase in ability or power. This man's power to accumulate wealth, therefore, will diminish; and besides, he will discover that since his real mind is barren he cannot enjoy the wealth he has produced.

Happiness does not come from things, but from the appreciation of things, whether they be physical or metaphysical, real or ideal. Appreciation, however, is a flower that grows only in the garden of the finer mentality; therefore, he who has neglected the finer things in mind and thought has lost capacity for real enjoyment.

The mind that has visions, that dreams dreams, that lives largely in the ideal and that frequently soars to heights sublime may be looked upon as impractical or worthless, but it is such minds that have given us everything in life that is worthwhile. The mind that explores the wonders and the splendors of the great within, that is, the higher and the finer fields of the mind—it is this mind that discovers music, art, literature and invention; and without these we would still be living in caves. In those same interior realms man finds philosophy, ethics, religion, metaphysics and science, and when he fully understands these he will be able to master himself and place the universe at his feet.

It is evident, therefore, that the path to greatness and the path to the doing of great things invariably leads directly into or through the great within, because it is in the vastness of interior mentality that we find all the limitless possibilities that are latent in man. He who would do things, therefore, that are really worth doing, must place his mind in perfect touch with the finer source of power, capacity and ability. In other words he must try to do things in the within as well as in the without. The possibilities of the within must be awakened and developed, and then practically applied in the field of tangible things.

In this connection, however, we must remember that the mind that acts solely upon the within is no better than the mind that acts solely upon the without. The vision must come first, but the idea that the vision reveals must be applied in real and practical life. When this inner capacity has been gained, or as it is being developed, all the power of that capacity must be utilized constructively in tangible life. What is not turned to use is wasted, and the mind that wastes its power will soon lose its capacity to produce power.

To become proficient in the new way of doing things we should work daily in the two worlds, the inner mental world and the outer practical world; the world of greater possibilities and the world of greater things; the world of ideals and the world of tangible results. There are thousands of minds that have discovered superior ideas in the larger fields of their mentalities, but they have taken no steps toward applying those ideas. And there are thousands with remarkable mental capacity who are making no use whatever of the powers of that capacity. These are minds that have begun to do things in the within, but have not begun to do things in the without. Therefore, no results of any value to anybody are forthcoming.

It is a fact that should be well remembered that no process of development has actually produced development until that power that is being developed can produce tangible results. In other words, no mental attainment is a permanent attainment until it can express itself in actual achievement. On the other hand, no great achievement is possible until the corresponding attainment has been developed, and since attainment constitutes inner mental capacity, power and ability, while achievement constitutes the actual producing of external results, it is evident that the doing of things, both in the within and in the without is absolutely necessary.

Every day should have its visions as well as its tangible deeds. Certain periods should be given every day to the concentration of attention upon the great within with a view of awakening new possibilities of mind and thought. And every day these new possibilities should be worked out in actual use. He who would do things—things worth doing—and who would continue to do greater and greater things, must live a whole life and not simply a half a life. That person, however, who lives only in the practical is living only one-half of his present sphere of existence, though the same is true of him who lives only in the world of visions and dreams. The life that is full and complete—the life worthwhile—the growing life—is the life that dwells both in the subjective and in the objective; that develops daily the limitless powers of the great within, and that applies those powers every day in the great without. It is such a life that does things that are of real value both to the individual and to the world; it is such a life that has found the new way of doing things, and it is such a life that will ever continue to do greater and greater things.

11

HOW GREAT GAINS ARE REALIZED.

Though it may seem paradoxical, nevertheless it is true that the man who works for himself alone is not working for himself alone. For the fact is that the more you are concerned about your own personal gain the less you will accomplish, and the less you accomplish the less you gain. Great gains come through great achievements, but great achievements do not come through the mind that has no higher goal than the working out of a mere personal aim. The man who works for a great idea, even to the extent of forgetting personal gain is doing more to promote personal gain than he could possibly do in any other manner. On the other hand, the man who works for a great idea solely because he knows he will secure personal gain thereby is not working exclusively for his own gain. His own gain may be his original purpose, nevertheless before he goes very far he will find himself promoting the gain of the entire race.

Proceed with a great idea in view and you will do more for yourself than you could do through any other course. But in any case what you are doing for yourself will be insignificant compared with what you are doing for the race. Therefore no person can be called selfish who is promoting a great purpose in the world. Though his personal gain may be large still he is giving more to the world in proportion to his gain than any other person whose purpose in life is of a lesser degree.

The man who carries out a great idea benefits everybody, therefore does not work solely for himself ; but the man who has no other aim than to get something for himself does not benefit anyone, not even himself. And the reason why is found in the fact that when you are working solely for yourself you are placing in action only a very small part of yourself.

Work for a great idea and you arouse great ideas in your own mind. Great ideas produce great thoughts and great thoughts produce great men. Therefore the man who thinks great thoughts must necessarily become a greater man, and the simplest way for anyone to form the habit of thinking great thoughts is to work for a great idea. When you work simply for yourself or for your own personal gain your mind will seldom rise above the limitations of the undeveloped personal life; but when you are inspired by some great purpose, some extraordinary project, all your thoughts break bounds; your mind transcends limitations; your consciousness expands in every direction; and you find yourself in a new world, a great world, a wonderful world; dormant powers, faculties and talents become alive, and you discover yourself to be a larger man by far than you ever dreamed yourself to be.

Whatever your present work may be have some great purpose in view. Never permit yourself to settle down to mere prosaic existence. Dream of extraordinary attainments and do all you can both physically and mentally to move forward now toward that superior goal that your visions have revealed to your mind. Never be dissatisfied with temporary conditions in the present and do not resist what appears to be fate, but do follow the light of the greater vision no matter where it may seem to lead.

When you are so situated that there seems to be no opportunity for advancement do not imagine that nothing but an ordinary life is in store for you. Have a great idea in view; think of it, dream of it, work for it, live for it. Enter so completely into the superior world of that great idea that all your thoughts become extraordinary thoughts. Gradually you will grow into the likeness of the great thoughts you think, and ere long you will become so large that you will break the shell of your present limitations. Then you will find yourself in a new world where opportunities are so rich and so numerous that you cannot possibly use them all.

There are worlds and worlds of opportunities all about us that are waiting for men and women who are sufficiently competent to take advantage of them. Therefore make yourself a little larger than you are and you will receive a thousand welcomes from those worlds. But first you must begin to think great thoughts, and great thoughts can originate only in that mind that lives for something infinitely larger than the personal self. You cannot bring out the greatness within you, unless your purpose in life is so large, so vast and so immense that all the elements of your being are drawn irresistibly toward the supreme heights of unequalled attainment.

The present may seem to hold nothing in store for you, but that need not concern you in the least. Work for a great idea. If you cannot work for it in the real, work for it in the ideal; but do work for the greatest ideal that you can possibly picture, and work for it every moment of your existence. You will thereby enlarge, expand and develop your mind constantly and ere long you will find yourself in the company of those who have been chosen for greater things. No matter how empty the present may seem to be there is a way out, and to find the way out simply follow the light of some great idea.

To work for a great idea is to work yourself up toward the greater, the larger and the superior m all things, and you will not continue this upward movement very long before you enter the great world of opportunities. Then you may choose what you would do, where you would go and what kind of a life you prefer to live. The drawing power of a great idea is irresistible. Place yourself in the strong current of this power and you will positively move toward greater and better things. To think great thoughts occasionally, however, is not sufficient. Every mind has moments when consciousness soars to empyrean realms, but those moments are not numerous in the average mind, and in most instances they are purely sentimental. They are not inspired by some great purpose or some extraordinary project that we have resolved to carry out; therefore, they do not awaken the greatness that is within us, nor do they call forth the limitless powers that are latent in the superior nature of man.

To produce the results we have in view our great thoughts must be in the majority, and they must be animated with a deep, strong desire to reach the very highest heights that the mind can possibly picture. We are not thinking great thoughts unless we are thinking the greatest thoughts that we can possibly create, and we are not working for a great idea unless we are working for the greatest idea that the most lofty moments of the mind can possibly reveal.

We may now be engaged in a great work, we may now be connected with a great enterprise where opportunities for advancement are very large and numerous, but that is no reason why we should be satisfied to keep our minds in the circumference of that enterprise. In fact, no matter how large the world in which you may be living now, if you wish to expand and develop your mind you must fix your attention upon a still greater world. No matter how large your present opportunities may be, if you wish to become a greater man than you are you must work for a far greater purpose than that which your present opportunities can possibly contain. Wherever you are, in a small world or a large world, have something greater still and you will invariably rise in the scale.

Do not be content to continue as you are, even though you have gained all your wants, because beyond what appears to be everything worthwhile to you, there is more, and this more is for you. When you are working for a great idea, everything that comes to you as a natural product of that great idea is your own, no matter how much it may be. You have not deprived anyone of anything through your efforts. Besides, what you are gaining, others may gain in the same way. The riches of the universe are limitless and any mind that begins to work for greater things will soon work up into greater things, and in the world of greater things there is always abundance. Quantity is unlimited, quality is unsurpassed and perpetual increase is the law. Realizing these facts, do not work simply for yourself. Work also for the greatest idea that your mind can possibly picture. You will thereby scale the heights and in consequence will do more for yourself than you possibly could in any other manner. In addition, you will add immeasurably to the welfare of the world.

In this same connection there is another idea that should be noted and applied with care, and it is the correct idea concerning the minding of one's own business. To succeed in any business, it is necessary to mind that business properly, but no man can mind his own business properly so long as he minds no business save his own. He who knows nothing but his own specialty does not know his own specialty; and he who finds interest in one thing only has too small a mind to know what that one thing really is. The larger and broader your mind the better you can care for your own business, and to broaden your mind, be interested in the progress of all good business. Do not divide your attention, nor scatter your forces, but live in that lofty mental world where you can have a comprehensive view of all things at all times.

The small, narrow, submerged mind can see nothing but his own, therefore fails to do much with his own because every part depends more or less upon the whole. The large mind, however, can grasp the elements of everything that is conducive to growth, advancement and success, and naturally incorporates those elements in his own special work. The man who would succeed in the largest and the best sense must enter into the consciousness of universal success. That is, he must place himself in touch with everything that does succeed, and must enter into the life of that power that is back of every successful enterprise. But he cannot do this unless he takes an active interest in the best and the largest success of everybody.

To take a real interest in the success of everybody is to develop a strong desire for the success of everybody, and the stronger our desire for the success of others the stronger becomes that power that produces success in ourselves. There are few things that are more potent in the awakening of power than that of a strong desire for the results of that power. Therefore a strong and constant desire for the greatest possible success for everybody will naturally develop in ourselves the largest measure of that power that makes for a great success.

When we mind nothing but our own business we call into action only a small part of the mind, but when we take a living interest in all business we call into action practically every part of the mind. New power is thus awakened, and if our concentration is good we can turn all of that new power into our special work, thus adding remarkably to our actual working capacity. It is therefore profitable in a certain sense to mind everybody's business, that is, to keep your mind in sympathetic touch with everybody's business. But it is not only profitable, it is the mark of real manhood. To be deeply interested in the welfare of others is an indication of superiority, and to give a great deal of thought to the promotion of the welfare of others is a means toward the development of superiority.

The man who minds his own business only is a very small man, and his world is so shallow and contracted that he will gain very little of those things in life that are really worthwhile. Though he may gain riches he will not gain the power to appreciate what riches can procure, which is highly important because we can enjoy only that which we can appreciate; and it is only the large lofty mind that can appreciate the real worth of those things that actually add to the value and joy of life.

In minding the business of others, however, we must not meddle or interfere. Each individual is free to do his own work in his own way, but whenever we can improve the conditions that surround the work of the individual we should count it a privilege to do so. We are our brother's keeper in a certain sense, and we shall find that if all work in harmony trying to promote the welfare of each individual, the whole of the race, as well as each part, will be far better off than when we all work singly, trying to reach our own selfish goal, regardless of what happens to others.

To develop the individual is the supreme purpose, and to give to each individual all that he has earned or produced, no matter how much larger it may be than that of anyone else, is the true principle of justice. But both the development of the individual and his personal gain can be promoted to far greater advantage when he works in harmony with all, trying to add to the welfare of all.

The man who cares only for himself may gain the possession of things, but he will lose those elements of mind and soul through which he can enjoy things, and instead of promoting his progress he will retard it. Selfishness has the tendency to contract; therefore the selfish mind becomes smaller and smaller until its capacity both for work and happiness is reduced to nothing. The man, however, who cares for everybody will live in the universal and will enter into harmony with powers that are limitless. He will thereby not only gain possession of more things and better things, but will also gain the conscious appreciation of the finer elements of things; and it is this consciousness that gives true richness and true happiness to life.

There is no life that is greater or more beautiful than the life that has lived in the universal, that is, in the highest and deepest sympathetic touch with every person, with every enterprise and with every ideal. Such a life will expand and develop all the powers of the mind and make man great indeed; and the great mind will attain much, achieve much, gain much and enjoy much. This universal sympathy, however, must not be sentimental. It must be strong and constructive and must aim, not only to add to the welfare of everybody, but also to gather from every source the very best that we can use in our own individual world. It must be a mutual giving and receiving on the largest possible scale. In that manner everything that comes into life may be as large in quantity as we may desire, and as high in quality as we can appreciate and enjoy. Thus the present moment will be full and complete, and the greatest gains both in thoughts and in things will be realized.

12

THE PSYCHOLOGICAL MOMENT.

When all the elements of those circumstances, conditions, forces, environments and opportunities that surround a personal life are about to meet in a favorable climax, we have what is called the psychological moment. It is psychological because the interior powers, the higher powers, the superior powers—in brief, the best powers that are active at the time are on the verge of gaining a decisive victory over limitations and things. At such a moment the mind and soul approach the superior and all the elements and forces concerned are ready to obey. All things pertaining to the exterior have been drawn into the onward current of those things that act from the interior and everything is about to give up its power for the promotion of the predominating purpose.

When all things in your life have come to that state where they can work together for you and bring about a speedy realization of your leading object in view, then you have entered the psychological moment. What to do at such a time is of the utmost importance. ' If you can properly handle the psychological moment the dreams of your life will come true, but if you cannot, years and years of hard work may be lost, and much of it will have to be done over again.

A psychological moment comes to races, to nations, to armies, to parties, to communities and to every individual person who is alive with some definite purpose in view. To find the cause of the psychological moment is not always possible, but it is usually an effect of much thought and effort along a certain line combined with present powers and such conditions as predominate at the time. The psychological moment can therefore be produced by anyone who knows how and who will take the time. And everybody should learn how, and should take the time, because it is only through the psychological moment that really great things are done at the right time.

When the psychological moment comes the time is ripe for your particular action. The world is ready to appreciate what you intend to do, and all the forces and elements of life are at hand to aid you to a successful issue of the great undertaking you have in mind. To take advantage of the psychological moment is to do things at the right time, when everybody wants you to do it, and when everything wants to help you do it.

The importance of paying attention to the psychological moment is very evident when we know that thousands of great things have been attempted before the race was ready to co-operate. And it was therefore seeds scattered upon stony ground where no results were secured. In like manner, thousands of great things have been attempted while the circumstances, forces and elements were adverse, and these through their adverseness perverted such actions as were applied; those actions, thereby, either became detrimental or were neutralized entirely.

When a great man has acted at the wrong time and has acted in vain, we find that instead of becoming a great light in history he has either been absolutely forgotten or is remembered only with contempt. It may sometimes seem difficult, however, to wait for a great moment, but it is better to wait and then do something of worth than keep on trying at the wrong time and never accomplish anything. But when we speak of waiting for the psychological moment we do not mean that that moment will appear of itself at a certain time to every individual. On the contrary, it is something that we ourselves must create. Therefore, if we have some great purpose in life we should begin at once to create the psychological moment through which that purpose can be brought forward and realized to the very highest degree.

We cannot single handed make the world over, and we cannot at once make the race appreciate our efforts, but we can gradually bring ourselves into such perfect harmony with the world that all will appreciate our efforts in a measure. And we can gradually bring ourselves into such united action with all the elements and forces of life that all of these will come to our aid and work together to promote the purpose we have in view. The wise man will not try to force upon the world what the world cannot now receive. He will do now what can be appreciated now, and in the meantime he will enter into more perfect harmony with the world that all concerned may understand each other better.

The wise man will not undertake difficult things until he realizes that all the circumstances are ready to work with him, because he knows that if the circumstances are not ready to work with him he will fail. Therefore, instead of defying circumstances as so many do, the wise man proceeds to secure the cooperation of his circumstances. He enters into more perfect harmony with the powers that be. He meets half way those conditions that do not understand his purpose. When things will not go his way he goes their way for a while until a better acquaintance is secured; then all things are more than willing to go his way because they have discovered the superiority of his purpose in life.

Before we undertake anything we should prepare the way. We should secure the cooperation of all the elements of life and should secure the appreciation of the world in which we expect to act. In other words we should first create the psychological moment. Sometimes this moment can be produced in a short time, and then again it may take years. But what is time compared with such deeds as may change the course of the entire race and live for countless periods of time.

To produce the psychological moment, have a strong purpose and keep this purpose uppermost in mind regardless of what may be said or done. Believe that you can carry out that purpose in the fullness of time, and permit nothing to disturb that belief in the least. Hold fast to your belief as if it were life itself, until all thoughts and actions come to recognize that belief as supreme. Whenever any purpose in your life comes to be recognized by your thought as supreme, all thoughts and all actions will begin to work for the promotion of that purpose. Everything in your life will move in the direction of that purpose and will help you work toward the goal in view. And when all your thoughts begin to work for a certain great purpose all your circumstances will begin to move in the same direction, gradually giving more and more power to the good work and steadily becoming more and more favorable.

The stronger you become in your determination to promote that purpose the stronger will be your life and your thought moving in the same direction.

And the more power your personality applies in this direction the sooner will all your circumstances and environments fall into line and turn over all their powers to you. We all know that this is true and we all know why. No further analysis therefore is required, but the fact that such is the case is of enormous importance to us. A strong soul with a powerful mind, living, thinking and working for the promotion of a great and worthy purpose, will soon cause all the elements and forces in his life move toward the great climax. It will not take him long to turn fate, to transform adversities, to change tendencies and thus cause all the powers of his life to work with him and for him. To him the psychological moment will soon come and when it does come he can fulfill his great purpose and cause his cherished dream to come true. It is in this way that great deeds are done, deeds that never die, but that continue as endless inspirations to all the world.

Many minds set out with great aims in life, but they do not continue faithfully. They lose courage and often cease for years to work for those aims; but the psychological moment does not come in this way. It does not come by itself. It is something that we must create. It is the climax of months or years of thought and effort in a certain direction. Therefore, if we permit our high purpose to rest, nothing will be done toward producing psychological moment for that purpose. The great moment comes when we have marshaled all the powers within us and about us, and brought them all together ready to act at once and in unity in giving their all to the purpose we are just about to fulfill.

When all the elements, forces and circumstances in a person's life are brought together and made to act in perfect unity, and at the right time and place, it is evident that nothing can prevent that person from doing something great and very remarkable. The average person seldom acts under favorable circumstances and hardly ever secures the co-operation of all the forces in his life. Great deeds, therefore, cannot be expected through his efforts.

To produce the psychological moment have a great purpose and live constantly for that purpose no matter what may transpire. Bring every thought and action into unity with that purpose as rapidly as you can and steadily direct all the powers of your being to work for the coming of the great day. Circumstances and environments will soon respond to your irresistible determination and will soon go with you turning all their energies upon the one purpose in view.

A resolute determination that cannot be shaken, combined with high aims, abundance of faith and positive actions—these are factors that will bring the psychological moment to anyone and bring it quickly. But we must bear in mind that after we have chosen our purpose we must live, think and work for it constantly, and not fall back for a single moment. When you establish a strong tendency in a certain direction everything in your life will soon establish the same strong tendency and when all these tendencies are speeding forward, aiming at the same goal, the climax will soon come. Then you are in the psychological moment, all things are ready to act upon your word, and through their united action they will be fully able to do that for which they have assembled. The moment may not last long—a few days, a few weeks, or at times a few months. Frequently such moments last but an hour, but in great undertakings that involve many circumstances the time is usually prolonged to several months, or years.

When the moment has come, however, you must act and act properly or the efforts of years will be lost. All things have come your way, not to do something unbeknown to you, but to do something for you. And that something must correspond with the original purpose that brought about the psychological moment. It need not be exactly the same purpose, but it must be a kindred purpose. When the great moment appears you may discover that you can act to better advantage by turning all your energies toward a slightly different plan, but this plan must be in harmony with the original idea or the forces assembled cannot assist you. However, you must act and act in the best manner that you possibly know and this is especially true with regard to the actions of your mind. As you think at this time so will be your interior forces, and as your interior forces are, so are those forces that act in your environment. All things, therefore, have come to follow your word, but without your word or action they can do nothing.

To do the best thing possible at this time have unlimited faith in yourself. Have unlimited faith in everybody that is in any way connected with the purpose in view, and have unlimited faith in all the opportunities, conditions and circumstances that now are with you. View everything from the very highest place you can reach. Be your best. See yourself at your best and think of everything as it is while at its best. Do not criticize anything or anybody. Your object is to get the very best out of this great opportunity and you must not burden the mind with a single adverse thought. If you are not doing your work as well as you wish, or if others are not proving themselves equal to your high ideal give no thought to this deficiency. You will certainly take a long step forward when this moment is finished, and others will do likewise, but every critical thought will act as an obstacle to the greatest results.

Place yourself in the highest and the most harmonious relationship with all things. You must meet everything on the mountain top, because if you are on the heights all your helpers will come up also, and will thus produce that which is rare, worthy and superior. During the psychological moment you are the great master of the situation. As you go so will everything about you go because all things have come to go your way. What you want done that will be done because all things have come to act upon your word. It is therefore of the greatest importance that you occupy a very high place in thought, purpose and action. You must appear at your best, feel your best and recognize your own real superiority.

Your own thoughts become patterns and must therefore be supremely high. Your own actions determine the action of mighty forces and creative powers and must therefore be in harmony with all that is lofty, perfect and true. Do not for a moment lose sight of your purpose, and in the midst of the great moment be more determined than you have ever been before to gain the great goal.

When the psychological moment is approaching many minds make it a practice to relax their efforts, blinking that since things are coming their way the results will be forthcoming without any further personal attention; but this is a serious mistake. Things are coming your way because you have drawn them into your path and they are coming to carry out what you wished to have done when the climax comes. If you leave the field of action the great assembly will have no leader and can therefore do nothing. Accordingly they will soon scatter and you will have lost one of the great opportunities of your life. Thousands of minds have left the field of action at the approach of the great moment, believing that things would come right because indications pointed toward a favorable climax. Thus they lost completely because they did not recognize the psychological side of the moment. And it is the psychological side that is the one most important side.

When this great moment comes all things in your life are brought together to obey your will. And you must be in the very midst of all these things to give the proper word of command. Therefore, when the great climax is approaching have more faith than you ever have had; be more determined than you ever were, and think higher thoughts than you ever thought before. Though you are not to criticize others at the time, still you must bring yourself up to the very highest point of perfection possible. The higher you are in the world of power, superiority and worth the greater will be the results when the expected climax does come. Depend, therefore, upon higher power and relate yourself harmoniously to the Supreme.

Try to fed that you are being filled and surrounded by forces that come direct from the very presence of the Supreme and that it is therefore impossible for you to fail. Do not permit yourself to fall down at any place nor fall short at anything. It is the time for you to attain and achieve as you never did before, and nothing in your personality must stand in the way. While the psychological moment continues, special attention should be given to a pure life, a strong life, an ideal life and a masterful life, and all the qualities and attributes of perfection should be constantly in mind.

Live in the upper story, but act upon the tangible world according to the high purpose that you are determined to fulfill. The results will be as you wish. The goal will be gained. Then you can proceed to prepare the way for a still greater psychological moment, and thus in the coming days reach a much higher goal than you have ever known before.

13

THE POWER OF PERSONAL APPEARANCE

Among; the many things that determine what places in life men and women are to occupy, the power of personal appearance is one of the greatest, and frequently by far the greatest. Although it is ability that counts in the long rim provided that ability is applied to the best advantage, still there is a great deal of ability that is so completely hidden back of an unattractive personal appearance that it is never recognized nor given its legitimate opportunity. Where we find exceptional ability we also find exceptions to this rule, but there are thousands and thousands of brilliant minds, and any number of minds not quite as brilliant, that are handicapped constantly and most seriously on account of deficiencies in their personal appearance.

We all know this to be the truth. The subject is therefore worthy of the most thorough attention because no one can afford to permit anything to stand in his way. The best use of the best that we possess must be our purpose and everything necessary to fulfill this purpose should be supplied.

The term "personal appearance,^' however, does not refer simply to dress or manners, though these are important, and everyone should make it a point to be dressed as attractively as possible. But aside from these it is the appearance and the expression of the human face that really determine the final results. To this end the face of the man should be strong and expressive and the face of the woman should be beautiful and expressive.

In the business world the man with the strong face is invariably given the preference. He will be selected for the most responsible positions if he is working for others, and if he is working for himself he will be far more successful than his negative faced neighbor because the public is irresistibly attracted to the man who produces the best and the strongest impression.

No matter how able you may be if you do not produce a good impression upon the world your remarkable ability will not serve you as well as it should. On the other hand, when you do produce a good impression, all of your ability will be in demand, and will be called forth to the best advantage, not only to yourself, but to everybody concerned. And since there is nothing that can produce a better impression than a strong, expressive face every man will find it most profitable to develop such qualities or characteristics in his facial expression.

The man with the strong face will forge to the front in his world and the woman with the beautiful face will forge to the front in her world, provided that expressiveness is added to strength and beauty in each case. These are facts. It is there-fare of the highest importance to those who wish to press on to greater and better things to understand how personal appearance in this regard can be cultivated to the highest possible degree.

Every man should have, and may have, a strong, expressive face. Every woman should have, and may have, a beautiful, expressive face. The methods for such development are well known so that it is only necessary to understand and apply them.

To improve the form and the expression of the face will require considerable time and attention in most cases, especially where the essentials are still in an undeveloped state. But these essentials can in every case be brought forth, and every person can accordingly develop in his face the qualities and the expression that he may desire. There are a number of men and women, however, whose facial expressions are so near to the strong or the beautiful state of expression that they would only have to be touched up, so to speak, to make them exactly what they ought to be. These people, therefore, can in a very short time, demonstrate concisely that a decided improvement in facial expression can be secured, while those who may need further development can through the same methods accomplish the same results if sufficient time is allowed.

We meet hundreds of women every day whose faces have an ordinary appearance at first sight, but most of these faces upon closer examination will be found to contain all the essentials to beauty of expression; and though these essentials are so near to the surface as to be almost in evidence, still they are not harmonized and therefore continue to remain ordinary in appearance; they could, however, with a few slight changes be made decidedly attractive. These women fail to produce the favorable impressions that they might produce and consequently are at a disadvantage, both in the social world and in the business world. The places they deserve in the woman's world they do not secure because they do not appear as they really are, and the world usually judges according to appearances. This being true, we must take the world as we find it. And we must not hide what light we may possess nor permit undeveloped or perverse personal appearance to so mince matters for us that our superior qualities seem to produce inferior impressions.

In like manner, we meet hundreds of men every day whose faces are weak in general appearance, and there is nothing expressive about their personalities. We are not favorably impressed by them and usually conclude that they are just ordinary men, no more. But when we look closely at those faces we find remarkable possibilities of strength and power, possibilities so near to the surface that a few slight changes in the expression of the face would make them exceptionally strong. Many of these men are able, but they have not as a rule the opportunity to fully apply their abilities in the positions they now occupy and on account of their weak, negative faces they do not produce the desired impressions when they seek those opportunities elsewhere. In consequence, they continue in small, poorly paid positions when they really have the ability to do far better. We are all personally acquainted with hundreds of men in this very condition, and if we should investigate we should find thousands more.

In the meantime, from every part of the commercial world comes the call for competent men, men who can do things, men who can do greater things, and do them better than they have ever been done before. This being true, do not hide your ability behind a weak, negative face. Give your power expression so that the world can see what is in you at first sight. The world is too busy to take men on trial or upon anybody's say so, and we must be prepared to meet the world the way we find it. The man who can prove in the least time that he is able to make good will be given the preference in every case. When there are larger places to fill, he will be selected even though there are thousands of applicants all as able as he may be but not prepared to prove at sight what is in them.

The world is constantly looking for good men, therefore if you know that you are one of these, bring your power and your ability into your facial expression. In other words, let the light of your mind shine. The highest places are always given to the most brilliant mind.

There are thousands of men that would be promoted within a month if they would begin today to transform their weak, negative faces into strong, positive faces, and there are thousands of women who would in a short time win the various positions and the affections which they so earnestly desire if they would aim to bring to the surface the charm and the beauty that they actually possess. These are facts—^great facts—facts with which we are all familiar. How the man may develop the strong, expressive face and how the woman may develop the beautiful, expressive face will therefore be knowledge of priceless value.

We do know that men with strong faces and women with beautiful faces forge to the front, and we all desire to forge to the front. What is more it is not only our privilege to do so, but to be just and true to ourselves we must do so.

To proceed with the development of the strong, expressive face, begin by eliminating all negative states of mind such as fear, worry, depression, discouragement, lack of self-confidence, lack of push, instability, indifference, inertness and negativeness. Remove these by giving a strong facial expression to poise, determination, positiveness and soul. In other words cultivate the positive qualities and be determined to express them in every fiber of your personality. No forceful expression, however, must be permitted. The proper expression is that expression that inwardly feels great power and that applies that power in perfect poise. When you concentrate a strong, well poised expression through every part of your face think deeply of what you are in ability, capacity and power; that is, place the stamp of your real worth upon every thought you think while this concentration is practiced.

There are few things that will give more strength, more quality and more expressiveness to the expression of the face than to feel the power of real, genuine worth in every cell of the face and to hold that power in strong poise while it is being felt. It is also highly important to give a positive expression to your face at all times, and to give all the quality and worth that you can to that expression. This will not only stamp your face with strength and ability, but it will tend to bring forth more ability from the subconscious mind, and thus develop added ability at the same time.

Train your mind to express its very best in every part of your facial expression; that is, express yourself consciously and feelingly in your face so that everybody can see you, the real superior YOU, by looking^ at your face; because if the world can see you and what is in you in this ready manner you will positively be given the place you deserve.

To permit the mind to express its real worth through the personal appearance of the face in particular and through the entire personality in general, all wrong mental states must be entirely avoided, because all such states misdirect and confuse mental expression thereby producing false and undesirable impressions. The most detrimental of these states are fear, anger and worry and their various modifications. Fear always weakens the face as it is the most negative of all negative states, while anger and worry give the face a hard and ugly appearance. The same is true of all ugly mental states. Think ugly thoughts or permit yourself to feel disagreeable again and again and both beauty and the strength of your face will disappear if you ever had those qualities.

The beautiful face is produced by harmony of mind, sweetness of thought, love, tenderness, mental sunshine, joy, kindness and an inward feeling of the SOUL of the beautiful. Train yourself to feel the beautiful in your own soul and consciousness; then train yourself to express that feeling in your face, and your face will not look ordinary nor unattractive anymore. Instead, it will begin to express more and more of the loveliness of that charm that is always irresistible.

To change mental states and mental expressions from the wrong to the right, from the weak to the strong, from the negative to the positive and from the unattractive to the beautiful, is to remove gradually but surely everything that is cheap, ordinary, coarse, common or undeveloped in your facial expression. Your appearance, therefore, will no longer be a cheap edition but will become an edition de luxe, so to speak, and will in time become sufficiently attractive to win the admiration of the most idealistic mind.

That the expression of the face may be remarkably improved through the cultivation of the proper mental states is a fact that everybody will admit. And those who realize the importance of improving personal appearance in all respects will proceed at once with the application of these simple methods. But that the form of the face can be changed or even modified is an idea that will be doubted by many. Doubts, however, on this subject need not be entertained because experiments in physiological psychology have demonstrated that the form of the face can be largely changed, modified and improved. And the law through which this is effected has been called the law of subjective concentration.

The principle of this law is, that when you concentrate the mind upon any part of the body while the mind is in the subjective state, that is, a state of deep feeling, there will be an increase of vitality and nourishment supplied to that part of the body, and development of the cell structures will take place to a degree. That the form of the face, therefore, might be largely modified and improved through this method is evident, and especially since the mind concentrates more readily upon the face than upon any other part of the body. This idea, however, is one that will necessarily involve a great deal of practice, but everybody is advised to test it thoroughly if they feel that for any reason a modification in the form of the face is desired.

However, the application of this idea is by no means necessary to the improvement of personal appearance, because the simple methods presented above, that is, with respect to changing the states of the mind, and by cultivating a positive, expressive attitude at all times, will prove sufficient to produce almost any change that we have in mind in this respect. The principle is, to make the facial expression strong and expressive in the man, and beautiful and expressive in the woman. Because as we already know such facial expressions are of immense advantage, both in the social world and in the business world.

14

THE USE AND CULTIVATION OF PERSONAL MAGNETISM.

We all know that the human personality is more or less charged with magnetic and electrical forces, and it is becoming more and more evident to the Students of the psychological side of personal life that those forces have a distinct purpose in promoting the increase of ability and power in man, and that they can be increased indefinitely both in quantity and effectiveness. That man is an electrical battery, so to speak, and that he is more or less a living magnet, is a fact that no intelligent person will any longer dispute. That fact has passed from the world of doubt and has been accepted by the world of science.

It is therefore unnecessary to give time and space trying to prove that there is such a thing as personal magnetism. We all know that such a power does exist in us all and that it is worth a fortune to possess an exceptional degree of this power. What we wish to know, however, is how to use this power properly and how to make it much stronger than it is because we have found its value to be extraordinary to say the least.

In the use and cultivation of this power the first principle to be fully established in the mind is, that personal magnetism can be used upon yourself alone, and that its function is to promote the best possible expression of all the active qualities in your own personality; or in other words, to heighten an effect of everything you may do.

The belief that personal magnetism is intended for the influence of others is absolutely untrue, and what is more, such a thing is impossible. You cannot use this power to any extent in controlling others: it will not work that way. Should you attempt to influence others with this power you will not only fail to exercise any perceptible influence, but you will also lose what personal magnetism you may already possess. If you cannot succeed in life without trying to influence others in promoting your success you do not deserve success; and what you may gain temporarily through force or persuasion is not earned. It is taken, and will not prove of any worth to you in the long run.

When you have something of value to give to the world the world will come and get it without being forced. Everybody is looking for the new, the better and the superior, and you have simply to announce the fact, that is, advertise. You will thus have no difficulty in disposing of your product as rapidly as you can produce it. It is the man who has nothing of value to dispose of who does not succeed. And a few of these have decided to try to force people to come and purchase what they do not want and what may not have any value. And they have imagined that personal magnetism was one of the secrets through which the public could be made to give up their money against their will; but in this they have been very much mistaken, and all who have employed such methods have utterly failed.

The underlying secret of success is, first, be of worth, second, do something of worth, and third, create something that has worth. When you have worth the world will want you. You will be in demand. When your work has worth your services will be in such demand that you will have more opportunities than you can take advantage of. And when your products have worth you will have to work to full capacity to supply the demand. These are facts, and being facts all attention and all personal power should be concentrated upon the cultivation of worth in all these respects. And in this connection we shall find personal magnetism to be indispensable.

You may have a great deal of ability, but how much you can accomplish through the use of that ability at the present time will depend upon how well that ability is expressed. The best qualities in our possession can be expressed to advantage, or the reverse. Great ability may appear at its best or at its worst, and the presence or absence of the electrical and magnetic forces of the personality determine which it is to be. The finest mind becomes stupid when emptied of these forces, while even an ordinary mind will become exceptionally brilliant, for the time being, when electrified.

We all know that we can at times bring ourselves up to a place where we are actually superior to our usual selves, and everything we do at such times proves to be a masterpiece. But why should we not be able to bring ourselves up to this superior state at any time when very important work is to be done. The fact is that we can, and no one should permit himself to undertake anything without first placing his entire personality in the best possible working condition. In other words, before your personality is called upon to act, it should be electrified and well charged with those forces that can bring all forces and functions up to their very best state of action. And to possess personal magnetism is to possess an abundance of those forces under conscious control.

To cultivate this fascinating power, the first essential is to fully establish in the mind the true use of this power. You cannot increase a certain power while you are constantly misusing what little of that power you may possess. And in this connection the first fact to be remembered is, that this magnetic energy is to be used upon yourself alone. It is not to be used in persuading others to do something for you, but should be used in making yourself more competent to do something for others. Having fixed this in mind, learn to feel deeply, and learn to live, think and act in poise.

Through the attitude of poise all the forces of the system are converted into what may be called the curve movements, and it is such movements of the electric or vital energies of the system that makes a person fascinating, charming, attractive and efficient. The opposite movements, or what may be called the zigzag movements, the broken movements, of the forces within us are weakening, because in such movements force is lost; and in a person without poise nearly all the forces in his system move more or less in a zig zag fashion.

The curve movements of energy are constructive and accumulative, and will constantly charge and recharge the system until the personality actually becomes a living magnet, animated and electrified in every atom. When you are filled with such a power you will give a high polish to everything you do. You will constantly keep yourself up to the very highest point of efficiency, and you will heighten the effect both of your appearance and your actions.

When we speak of curve movements or zigzag movements we do not refer to the physical movements of the body or the muscles. We refer only to the movements of the various electric and magnetic forces that act within the human personality.

To have a goodly supply of highly cultivated personal magnetism is to establish curve movements in all the forces of your personality, so therefore in every attempt we make to cultivate this power we should bear this fact in mind.

When the forces of your personality move in the zigzag fashion most of the electricity of your system is lost; that is, it is thrown off at the many sudden turns that your energies make while in that mode of action, and accordingly your system is not electrified. Your personality is thereby kept in a more or less emptied condition, and all your faculties are lowered in power and efficiency.

To develop this power it is not necessary, as a rule, to increase the supply of vital energy in the system in order to secure the desired results. Most of us are already well supplied with personal power, but we waste most of it through anger, fear, worry, nervousness, restlessness, despondency and lack of poise. These states of mind and modes of actions, therefore, must be eliminated and perfect harmony of mind and personality established. To proceed, it is only necessary to take the power we already possess and to train all the forces of the personality to move in curves, to which should be added a deep desire for personal expression.

And curve movements in the human system invariably follow the attainment of deep feeling and poise.

Depth of feeling brings consciousness into touch with the finer vibrations of our interior forces and thus enables us to act on that side of our personal power that pertains to the cause realm. And poise causes all those forces to move harmoniously, thereby bringing about the results we desire. The fact is, as soon as perfect poise is established in the system and a deep desire for personal expression is attained the power of personal magnetism will increase every day, provided, of course, that this power is never misused through wrong states of mind.

To be in poise, however, does not simply mean to be quiet. There are a great many people who seem to be quiet who have no poise whatever, and who are utterly devoid of personal power. And this is explained by the fact that poise is a state of mind and personality that we realize when peaceful actions and strong actions are combined. We are in poise when we are full of life and power, and at the same time cause that power to act peacefully and harmoniously. When you are in poise you can actually feel strong and mighty forces throughout your entire system. You are literally alive with power, but you are also perfectly serene. You fed like a dynamo, but everything in your entire system is under perfect control. There is nothing intense about your actions, for all is harmony and order but bade of that order there is the consciousness of immense power.

When you are in poise you do not simply feel strength, but you fed strong; and there is a difference. When you feel strength you simply feel power passing through your system, but when you fed strong you feel that you yourself are that power; it is not passing through you, but it is you. When this state is felt and felt serenity you are in poise, and you should watch closely how that state came about. When you find how it came about you have found the secret for gaining this power in yourself at any time, so that you may not only make poise a permanent possession, but you may constantly develop the magnetic powers of your personality to a greater and greater degree.

A number of methods have been given for developing personal magnetism, but few of them are of any value. The only essential is to gain perfect poise; to think, act and feel in harmony; and to desire deeply the full and harmonious expression of all the energies and forces in your personality. In brief, be personally alive and in poise at all times and you will develop more and more of this fascinating power.

15

HOW TO USE THE POWER OF DESIRE.

In the' practical application of the principles of psychology to the business world, the right use of desire becomes invaluable as the way this power is used determines largely what results are to be secured through any or every effort that is made; and the real truth concerning the great power of desire has been very well expressed in the statement, "We get what we desire and in just the measure of that desire"; and also, "We always get what we wish for if we only wish hard enough." But what it may mean to wish hard enough is the problem; and what it is that truly constitutes real desire is a question that few can answer for themselves.

To the majority a desire is a mere wish for something, a wish that may be weak or strong, deep or shallow according to the value of the object desired. But in any case the desire is looked upon as a mere feding in the mind, nothing more. There are a few, however, who have discovered that there is more in desire than a mere wish for the object desired, and it is these few who get what they wish for. By some, these people are called fortunate, and in a certain sense they certainly are. Those who have learned to get what they wish for are certainly fortunate. Others give them credit for extraordinary ability, which is also true, for though they may not have exceptional mental attainment in every case, still they have ability to use a power that the many know nothing about. By another group they are frequently accused of taking undue advantage of their fellow men, but this does not explain the secret of their success.

The man who has discovered the real power of desire can get what he wants without wronging anybody, and he will get what he wants no matter how adverse the circumstances, how great the obstacles, or how hopeless the aim.

The principle is this, whatever you wish for, wish hard enough and you will get it; but the act of wishing hard is quite different from what the average person may think it is. You do not wish hard enough for anything unless you make that wish thoroughly alive with all the life and power that you can possibly arouse. You do not place in action the real power of desire unless you give your desire soul—
^the deep, strong invincible power of soul.

When the force of your desire is just as deep as the deepest depths of your interior life, and just as strong as all the power that can possibly be contained in that life, your desire will be realized. In

other words, you will get what you wish for when all of you is in your wish. The reason why is simply understood as there is nothing mysterious or supernatural about the process through which these results are obtained. It is only a matter of using all the power you possess instead of a small fraction, and this is certainly important in the business world.

When you make up your mind to reach a certain goal or accomplish something you have in view, results will depend directly upon how well you use the real or inner power of desire. If your determination to succeed is shallow and superficial you will accomplish but little. On the other hand, if that determination is as deep as the depths of your own life you will arouse the deepest forces of your life, and these forces are not only powerful, but are positively irresistible.. That you should succeed with such powers at your command is therefore evident When you make up your mind in this deeper, stronger sense you are bringing out into action the strongest and best that is in you. You are deeply in earnest and you feel very deeply on the subject in hand. In consequence, your desire to succeed will actually stir the very depths of your soul. Your whole being will become alive, and when all the power that is in you is alive with the deep, positive desire of invincible determination,

there is no adversity or obstacle in existence that you cannot overcome.

Make yourself strong enough and great enough and there is nothing in the world that will not change its course in any manner required so as to serve the purpose of your supreme desire. And every person becomes strong enough and great enough when the deepest powers of his soul are aroused. There is more in you than you ever dreamed, and there are times when this more becomes so strong that you feel that you could master the universe. And these deeper feelings are not mistaken. Make yourself as strong as nature has given you the power to become and the universe will make way for any plan or project you may wish to undertake. The secret is to use all the power in your present conscious possession. You may not be required to develop more at the present time, because if you arouse what can be aroused now you will have sufficient for practically an3^ing you may wish to accomplish in the present.

Any person can do what he makes up his mind to do, or get what he wants, when he makes use of all the power he is conscious of; and all that power is invariably aroused when every desire is given soul. Bring out all your power and make your wish alive with all that power. Then you will wish hard enough. And when you wish in this manner you will get what you wish for. To state it differently, you get what you desire and in the full measure of that desire when your desire is crammed with all the life and all the power and all the soul that there is in you.

Failure comes from half-hearted desires accompanied more or less with doubt, or from those desires that are so shallow that they never arouse enough power to overcome a single obstacle. Success demands not only the power to do things, but also the power to surmount every obstacle that may be met, and the power to transform every adversity into a rich and rare opportunity. But such power does not come from shallow thinking and half-heartedness in feeling and desire. He who would gain the power to do what he wants to do must sound the depths of his being. He must learn to draw upon those deeper forces of his mind and soul that alone can give him all the power he may require or demand; but he can do this only by deepening his desire; that is, by giving his desire soul.

Every desire that is felt to the very depths of being touches the vastness and immensity of the great within. And the power of the great within is invincible. The real power of a deep, strong desire comes from the great interior life within us; therefore it is never crude in its actions. It is not mere animal will or the dominating force of physical determination; nor is it necessarily connected in any way with physical might and main. On the contrary, it is one of the most refined among all the forces in the system. It is actual soul force, but soul force is not something that pertains to some other state of existence, for it is the very life of every tangible force in the universe, physical or mental.

When you begin to arouse soul force you begin to draw upon the limitless, and all your faculties and talents will begin to outdo themselves. You are not only bringing out the best that is in you, but you are going farther still. You are going back of present capacity and arousing that something that can give perpetual increase to your capacity. Therefore, it is simply inevitable that you should accomplish what you have in mind and get what you wish for. No one can fail who applies the best that is in him. But back of the best there is more. We all know that there is. We all have had moments when we realized the limitless vastness of the great within. And when we think of it, something informs us that we can even now bring forth into actual use enough of this superior power to reach any goal we may have in view, or scale any height to which the mind can aspire.

Give the deep, strong, invincible power of soul to every desire and you will awaken those powers within you that can fulfill every desire. Desire greatness with the soul of desire and you arouse the

powers of greatness. Those powers are within you. They are positively there. It remains for you to bring them out. And you can if your desires are so deep that they stir the very depths of your innermost being. Desire changes for the better, and if that desire is as deep as your own life you will produce that change in your own life that is necessary to bring about such changes in your external world as you may have in view.

Create the inner cause and the outer effect will inevitably follow. Desire success with the deepest and strongest desire that you can possibly feel, and you will arouse those very powers within you that can produce success. Desire an ideal environment and you awaken those qualities in your own nature which, when applied, can produce or build up that richer and better environment into which you wish to enter. In consequence, you will ere long find yourself in such an environment because like attracts like, and from superior causes come superior effects.

And most important of all, you will, through the use of this law, cause yourself to become what you constantly desire to become. But all your desires in this connection must be deep and strong. They must actually thrill with feeling, life and soul, and must stir into positive action every power that is latent within you. There is enough creative energy and mental building material within you to make you a mental and spiritual giant Therefore, you need not hesitate to aspire to the very highest state that your mind can possibly picture. It is in you to become what you want to become, and what is in you can be brought out into positive action through the penetrating power of a deep soul desire.

Whatever your desire, never fail to give that desire your very life, your whole life and the full power of the deepest strongest, finest life that you can possibly arouse from the inexhaustible depths of your own soul. Do not simply express a wish, express more. And make this more as large, as high and as powerful as you can. Give your wish soul, not simply sentimental soul, but that expression of invincible soul that will press on and on to the goal in view, no matter what the obstacles may be. Make your wish alive and be so thoroughly in earnest that every atom in your being thrills with a positive determination to make that wish come true. But never attempt to use mere mental force.

The soul of desire is far deeper than mind and infinitely more powerful than mind. Try to feel this soul whenever you express the power of desire, and when you do feel it try to feel more and more of the real life of soul. Try to feel the finer elements and the finer forces that exist within all physical life and all mental life. Try to pass in consciousness from the realization of one grade of soul to the realization of deeper, finer and larger grades of soul until you are conscious of the immensity and the vastness of your own supreme within. Then you will know what it means to give the invincible power of soul to every desire. Then you will know why everything must change before the deep, determined power of such a desire. Then you will know why those who possess the secret of real desire invariably scale the heights even though the whole world be against them and every imaginable obstacle in their way.

16

HOW TO USE THE POWER OF WILL.

Among the many important discoveries made in recent times one of the greatest is this: that man has the power to change himself and his environment through the intelligent use of the laws and the powers of his own being; also that he can build health, character and ability to almost any degree desired; that he can remove from his life what is not conducive to his welfare and happiness; that he can gain possession of more and more of that which is conducive to his welfare and happiness; that the possibilities within him have no limitations whatever, and that there is evidently no end to what he can do in the growth and development of himself and the world in which he lives.

The principles of this discovery have been demonstrated by thousands. Results have been secured in every known field of life and human action. Some of these results have been so extraordinary as to appear miraculous, and accordingly, new philosophies and new systems of thought are taking shape and form with these results as cardinal doctrines, while the human world is changing more or less to harmonize with the new conception of man,

We no longer submit to things as they are. We no longer permit our minds to accept adversity in a meek and lowly spirit. We no longer think that we have to give up to what appears to be inevitable, because we have discovered that man holds the destiny of his own life in his own hands. Man is supreme in his own life and in his own world. This is a fact that we now know. He may therefore have his own way in practically everything. He may form his own ideals and make them come true. He may plan his own future and realize everything in general and most things in particular, as expected. He has the intellect to understand the principle and the power to apply the law.

But here we meet a great and perplexing problem. Among the many who have tried to understand the principle and apply the law, thousands have secured the results desired, but other thousands have not. They have either failed wholly or in part to produce those changes in themselves or in their environments for which they have labored so faithfully. They have seemingly done their part and have done it just as well as those who were more successful. Why they should fail may therefore seem difficult to understand, but the real reason is easily comprehended.

There are many powers in man, but there is only one power that has controlling power, and that power is the will. The purpose of the will is to control and direct all the other powers of man; that is, it should direct those powers so as to cause them all to do what we want them to do. Since there is no limit to man's inherent capacity, and since the subconscious cannot be exhausted, neither in quantity of power nor in varieties of power, it is evident that man can do with his life whatever he may desire, provided he can cause all these powers to do what he may wish to have done. And he can.

The controlling power of the will can cause any other power in man to do whatever the will may direct it to do. But this controlling power of the will must be used not simply to control for the sake of exercising control, but for the purpose of turning the other powers in man into those channels of action where the results desired may be produced. When man undertakes to change himself or his environments every power in his system must be directed to so act as to promote that change. And the first power to be so directed is the power of thought.

The mind is creative and its powers can create the change desired when properly directed. This is a fact, however, that is fully recognized by all who have taken up the science and art of applied idealism, and they have almost without exception given their mental powers the direction required. But they have in too many instances neglected to give that same direction to their other powers^ and here we find the cause of the failure.

To direct the mind to think and act along scientific and constructive lines is the first essential, but the power of such thought will not produce any change in man until his personality is directed to live and express those elements and factors that are contained within such line of thinking. The idealist wills to think, but does not always will to do. And the reason is that he believes that right action will invariably follow right thought. But this is not always true. Thought never becomes action unless the same will to think also wills to act.

The complete will, that is, the full use of the will, controls both thought and action and must act in both in order to produce results. The creation of a new idea is not necessarily followed by the expression of that idea; because the will that wills to create an idea does not will to express that idea unless so directed by the mind. Some minds naturally combine the will to think, with the will to act, and it is such minds that have such good results both in the science of applied idealism and in practical psychology frequently with but little effort.

Those minds that fail to secure external changes for the better after they have changed their thought for the better fail because they do not combine naturally the will to think with the will to do. In these minds the will is not fully applied; that is^ it may will to think the ideal, but it does not always will to work out the ideal in tangible action. But when the will is so trained that it invariably wills to do what it has willed to think, every change in thought will positively be followed by a corresponding change in external conditions.

Man is as he thinks, but he is not the product of all his thought. The only thought that gives formation to the character, the mentality and the personality of man is the thought that contains the will to express itself. All other thought therefore is useless, and to create thought and not give that thought the will to express itself is to waste both time and energy. The larger part of the thought created in the average mind is of this kind. It takes shape in the mind, but does not contain the will to work itself out into real tangible results.

The path to greater power of mind and personality, therefore, may be found first, in training the mind to think only constructive thought, and second, in giving every thought the will to act. Right thinking will produce right conditions in mind and body, only when the will to act is just as strong and just as deeply felt as the will to think.

Constructive thinking will promote the advancement of man both in attainment and in achievement whenever the desire to work out the ideal is just as positive as the desire to imagine the ideal. And all thinking that pictures the greater and better, and that is animated with a positive desire to attain the greater and the better, is constructive thinking. And all thinking is right that is based upon the principles that the ideal of everything contains the power to become real. But in applying this power it is the will that must be used in every instance whatever the purpose may be.

The power of the will is indispensable whether the action be physical or mental. We can do nothing until we will to do it, and what we wish to have done in any particular sphere of action, we must will to do in that sphere of action. What we wish to have done in the mind we must will to do in the mind. What we wish to have done in the body we must will to do in the body. What we do in one part of the system will not be duplicated in some other part unless we so will it. The power of thought will work itself out in personal life only when we will to convert that power into personal power. The ideal becomes real only when the characteristics of the ideal are acted out in the real.

The secret, therefore, is to act in the real as you feel that you are in the ideal. When you have seen the vision of the soul, will to make it come true in the body. You can. But do not try to will simply with the superficial side of will. It is through the controlling power of the will that you cause your other powers to do what you wish to have done.

And this controlling power may be found within what may be termed the soul of the will.

Give soul to your desire to act and the mind will act through the deeper, interior, or actual field of the will. In this way you will consciously apply the controlling power of the will and thus succeed in doing what you will to do. The controlling power of the will is a direct expression of the superior man within, and we must always bear this fact in mind— that there is a larger man within. This interior man is the real YOU, and is infinitely greater and more powerful than your outer personality. And it is upon this interior man that you must depend for results. Whatever you do, expect the interior man to produce results and give the interior man full credit for everything that is thus accomplished. In this manner you become more deeply conscious of the interior powers within you, and therefore can apply them to greater advantage.

The superior man within controls the controlling power of the will, therefore to will to do what we desire to do, we must give the superior man within the right of way. In other words, act as if you were the superior man within and you will feel that you are the superior man within. Then your greater power will act. You will place in action the controlling power of the will whenever you may desire to act, and thus you can readily do whatever you may will to do. Here we should remember that the other personality has no real will power. You own possession of real will power only when you begin to feel that you are the greater man within.

That power of will that can calmly, but absolutely, direct all the other powers in your being to do what you wish them to do invariably comes from the depths of your life. When your feeling of life is deep, therefore, and when that depth of life is calm and strong, then it is that you gain that power that contains controlling will power, and then it is that you can work out in tangible life every change for the better that you have produced in the mind. Many minds are so constituted that they naturally give the superior man within the position of supremacy. And it is such minds that secure the greatest results in every field of endeavor. Those minds, therefore, that do not naturally give the superior man the position of supremacy, and do not give the greater powers within full right of way must train themselves to do so. And all minds can.

There are greater powers within you than you have ever expressed before. If you will cause those powers to come forth more and more you will steadily and rapidly advance, no matter what your work may be. If you are so constituted that you naturally give those powers right of way, you will move toward the high places in mind whether you understand those powers or not. You will forge to the front because you can feel something superior within you that prompts you to press on and on, overcoming every obstacle and scaling every height.

You can secure the same results, however, by training your mind to become exactly similar m consciousness and action to those who naturally give the greater powers within the position nature intends them to occupy.

When you proceed to apply the science and art of practical psychology and try to produce changes for the better, both in the mental world and in the physical world, results will depend upon two things, and in the last analysis of these two are one. If the mind naturally gives the greater powers within the right of way, and naturally gives every thought the will to express itself in tangible action, you have combined these two essentials, and results will be forthcoming. When the superior man within is in action, the will to think and the will to act practically become one will, and every mental change is followed by a corresponding physical change. But no mental change can produce a corresponding physical change unless the new mental change contains the will to express itself. And since real will power is inseparably united with the superior man within, in fact, is the expression of the superior man within, it is evident that we must permit this interior man to come forth if we desire superior mental changes to come forth and produce corresponding physical changes.

To be so constituted that the greater man within is naturally given this prominent position is well, provided that tendency is cultivated, but if it is not cultivated we will have results, up to a certain point only, and there will be no further progress. It is not necessary, however, to be so constituted naturally in order to secure great results. The mind can readily be trained to work out into tangible life any new or improved condition that is realized in mind or consciousness. The will to think and the will to act can and must be made one will. And the power of creation and expression can be made so strong that the moment we discern an ideal we can begin to make it real.

In this entire study we should always bear in mind the great fact that what comes natural to some can be developed in all, and that the greatest results come, not to those who depend exclusively upon natural talent, but to those who take what they have, be it ever so little, and proceed with further development, never ceasing until they have realized the highest attainments of which they have dreamed.

We all have some will power. Whenever we move a muscle or utter a word we use the controlling power to carry out such actions. We can develop this function further and further until we can cause every power we possess to do what we may wish to have done. And we develop this function whenever we will to act out in the tangible any and every change for the better that we have pictured in the mind. The principle is to will to do whatever you have willed to think; and to will, not from the surface of your mind, but from the deepest depths of your mind. Thus you will become in the real what you desire to be in the ideal; and you will cause the vision of the soul to become a tangible reality.

We all have felt the power of the superior man within. We all have moments when we know that we are greater by far than the visible self ever appeared to be. And those moments can be made not only more numerous, but a constant realization. We can train ourselves to feel more and more of the greatness within and to express more and more of that greatness. We can do this by giving the larger interior man full right of way. We should proceed, therefore, to let the power that is within come forth. We should let it even take full possession of our entire personality. It will never lead us wrong, but will instead prompt us to press on and on regardless of circumstances until we reach the very highest heights we have in view.

Act as if you were this great interior man, think that you are, feel that you are, know that you are; thus you give the greater within you full right of way and the real YOU becomes supreme. Then you discover that it is all you, and that the all of

you is great indeed. Henceforth you can proceed to do in larger and larger measure what the modern mind has discovered that man can do; you can change yourself, improve yourself, advance yourself; grow out of any inferior condition into any superior condition; create health, harmony and happiness in abundance; live as you wish to live; become what you desire to become; increase perpetually your capacity to attain and achieve; build character and ability to the highest degree of efficiency and power; and place yourself upon that high pinnacle of being, where you can truthfully say. My life is in my own hands, and what my future is to be, I, myself, have the power to determine.

17

THE NEW MEANING OF GOOD BUSINESS.

The Statement is frequently made that it is good business to pursue such and such a course; in other words, that it is profitable in a financial way. And in the minds of many, anything is good business that is profitable financially; but the psychology of industrial life is proving conclusively that the man who is looking for financial profit must not look for financial profit alone. To achieve a real and lasting success the man of business must seek not only to build profit, but he must also seek to build himself. If his business has only financial profit in view the time will come when the business will be larger than the man; and it is the man who is smaller than his business that cannot stand prosperity. Success will turn his head and he will do something to spoil everything. He will thereby lose what he has gained, and being a small man he is very liable to go all to pieces when adversity comes. The large man, however, will not be disturbed by misfortune. He will begin again. He will turn his past experience into capital and will rise higher in the scale of achievement than ever before. But he will not lose his bearings when the greater success arrives.

He will grow with the growth of his business and will fully enjoy every step of the way.

A careful study of the industrial world proves conclusively that the majority of the failures in business life are due to the fact that the business man does not as a rule aim to grow with his business. When his sole aim is profit his business will grow for a while, but he will not. Sooner or later he will find himself too small for the further promotion of the enterprise, and when this stage is reached he will either lose his hold upon his business or lose his head. In either case things will begin to go wrong, and failure will follow.

The idea that business is business, regardless of its nature, and that anything is good business that promotes the growth of the business itself, will cause the business man to give his whole attention to methods for producing profit. He will ignore the principles of character and the laws of the mind, and will in consequence deteriorate as a man. His real ability will weaken and his future success, if he has any, will not be the result of business ability, but will be the result of shrewdness. Real ability creates, while shrewdness simply appropriates what others may have created. This, however, is not success, and no man who has respect for his own life, and regard for his future, will ever consider such a method for a moment

The man who tries to promote his business through questionable methods is harming himself. He is violating the laws of his own mind and is therefore retarding the growth of his own mind. But no person can afford to retard his own growth, because future success as well as happiness depends directly upon the growth of the mind, soul and character. If we wish to live a more successful life, a larger life, a worthier life and a happier life in the days to come we must continue to promote our own growth and personal advancement now.

To picture the next ten, twenty, fifty, seventy-five, or even a hundred years as a period of steady advancement in everything that is worthy, rich, beautiful and ideal is to look forward to a life that is certainly worth living, and such a prospect for the future will naturally fill a person's mind with unbounded gratitude to think that he is alive. But such a future cannot be realized unless a full and constant development of mind, character and soul is promoted now.

To build for greater things in any part of his life man must constantly build himself. Therefore he cannot afford to let anything, not even present financial profit retard his own growth. And financial profit secured through questionable means will retard his growth. In fact, the more profit he secures of this sort the smaller he himself becomes as a man.

There are only two ways through which financial profit can be gained; the one is through business ability practically applied, and the other is through any one or more of the illegitimate methods that are more or less in evidence in the business world. If you have no business ability of your own you cannot create success. Therefore, when a man who has no business ability succeeds, we know that he has appropriated the success that others have created. And the mere consciousness of such a fact will cause the mind of the individual who is guilty to dwarf and deteriorate.

The man who succeeds by appropriating the success of others has been told any number of times by moralists that he is harming his fellow men; but that argument does not impress itself very deeply on his mind because his answer is that others have the same privilege to do what he is doing. According to his logic there is no wrong in using any method whatever in building up his business so long as others are free to use the same method in building up their business; and with this argument he appears to make a strong case. In fact, he has convinced many of the best minds that business simply is business; that it has laws of its own, laws which have only one object in view, which is to build business ; and that whatever is conducive to the building up of business is good and legitimate in business.

There is, however, another side to this argument, and that side deals with the man behind the business. The man behind the business is the cause. The business itself is the effect. Therefore, what is bad for the man is bad in the long run for his business; and what is good for the man is good for his business. When he does something that decreases his ability and power his business will soon fed the effect, and will begin to go down; but when he does something to increase his ability and power, and continues in this course, his business will steadily grow until his success may become remarkable. This fact is self-evident.

We conclude, therefore, that the man who would win success that really is his own success, must aim to build up his mind while he is building up his business. And the building of these two can go together if his business methods are based upon principle, justice and character. But if he is using questionable methods his business will be an obstacle to the growth of his mind, and the reason why is simple. The mind cannot develop unless it is wholesome and works steadily along constructive lines; but no mind can be wholesome nor constructive in its actions that is engaged in an illegitimate enterprise. The mind cannot be straight so long as its work is crooked; and it is only the straight mind that can develop in ability and power, for it is only such a mind that can be in harmony with the laws of growth, development and advancement.

To promote its own development the mind must be true to itself, and just to its own laws. But no mind can be true to itself that is untrue to others. The mind that deals falsely with persons and things is dealing falsely with itself, and the mind that is dealing falsely with itself cannot develop itself. On the contrary, it is gradually destroying itself, and even a casual observation of things and persons about us will prove that this is the truth.

But there is another fact in this connection that is of equal importance. The man who depends upon his own ability to win success is using his own ability; and the more we use the ability we possess the more powerful and highly developed will that ability become. On the other hand, the man who depends upon shrewdness, speculation, games of chance and the like, is not using his business ability. In consequence, that ability will not develop, but will instead decrease in effectiveness and power. His abilities, talents and powers are not called into play; instead they are relegated more and more to the rear, and the man in consequence becomes less and less of a man. His success, if he has any, is not his own success. It was created by others, and justly belongs to the original creators.

The secret of greater and greater success is found in the development of greater and greater ability.

And to promote this development it is necessary to use the whole mind constructively and to make the fullest possible use of the ability we already possess. No destructive process therefore must exist in the mind, and no false action whatever must be permitted. The mind must be clean, wholesome, orderly, constructive and aspiring, and every action must aim to build the man while on its way to the building of things.

The man who would develop his ability must be true to himself and true to others. He must act upon principle and must desire the possession of that only that he is creating. He must employ only orderly, constructive and scientific methods because shady methods produce a shady mind, and such a mind will fail. It is therefore evident that no person can afford to establish his business upon any other foundation than that of principle, manhood and character. And it is also evident that the only business that is good business, is that business which tends to build the man while the man is building the business.